SALLY WISE is a bestselling author and a regular guest on ABC Local Radio in Tasmania. She has run masterclasses at the Melbourne Food and Wine Festival and The Agrarian Kitchen, and regularly holds cooking demonstrations and workshops at a variety of food festivals and community events. As a mother of six, Sally has perfected the art of transforming leftovers into new and delicious meals.

Other books by Sally Wise

Slow Cooker: Easy and delicious recipes for all seasons

*A Year in a Bottle: How to make your own
delicious preserves all year round*

*Out of the Bottle: Easy and delicious recipes for making and
using your own preserves*

*From My Kitchen to Yours: Delicious and gluten-free recipes
the whole family will love*

SALLY WISE

Leftover
Makeovers

Quick *and* fabulous food
from your fridge *and* pantry

ABC
Books

The ABC 'Wave' device is a trademark of the Australian Broadcasting Corporation and is used under licence by HarperCollins*Publishers* Australia.

First published in Australia in 2011
by HarperCollins*Publishers* Australia Pty Limited
ABN 36 009 913 517
harpercollins.com.au

HarperCollins*Publishers*
Level 13, 201 Elizabeth Street, Sydney NSW 2000, Australia
31 View Road, Glenfield, Auckland 0627, New Zealand
A 53, Sector 57, Noida, UP, India
77–85 Fulham Palace Road, London W6 8JB, United Kingdom
2 Bloor Street East, 20th Floor, Toronto, Ontario M4W 1A8, Canada
10 East 53rd Street, New York NY 10022, USA

National Library of Australia Cataloguing-in-Publication entry:

Wise, Sally.
    Leftovers makeovers : quick and fabulous food from your fridge
    and pantry / Sally Wise.
    ISBN: 978 0 7333 2940 1 (pbk.)
    Includes index.
    Cooking (Leftovers).
641.552

Cover photograph by Luke Burgess
Cover design by Mark Thacker
Typeset in Centaur MT 11.5/15pt by Kirby Jones
Printed and bound in Australia by Griffin Press
70gsm Classic White used by HarperCollins*Publishers* is a natural, recyclable product made from
wood grown in sustainable forests. The manufacturing processes conform to the environmental
regulations in the country of origin, Finland.

6 5 4 3 2   12 13 14 15

This book is dedicated to my family, who provide the inspiration
to continue a love affair in experimenting with food and
for their ever helpful suggestions along the way.

CONTENTS

ACKNOWLEDGMENTS

Thanks to my young friend Jo Leary, who was so helpful with taste-testing the recipes for this book.

Thanks also to Chris Wisbey for his enthusiasm and encouragement during the writing of the book.

INTRODUCTION

Leftovers can be a worry. We buy what we think we will need or what we fancy, or presume that our families will fancy, cook it up and then for a range of reasons it doesn't all get eaten. There might also be stray bits and pieces of vegetables lurking in the crisper drawer, and add to that the dregs, like peanut butter, tomato paste, honey and jam that lurk in the jars and tins in the fridge and cupboard, it all too often is easier just to throw it all out. What a waste of money. We all feel guilty about doing this, but a solution seems to escape us.

There is a better way though. Our grandparents would have been scandalised at our wayward ways with perfectly good food. I remember one of my grandmothers telling me how during the Great Depression of the 1930s she saw her father digging over the vegetable patch, hoping to come across a stray carrot or potato that had been missed in an endeavour to eke out the little food available to feed his family. She was thrifty forever after; a characteristic of her generation from which we perhaps could learn.

The issues for our society are even more far-reaching than the single fear of going hungry, though many scientists say there is ample evidence to suggest that significant shortages are, if not imminent, then at least inevitable.

A 2009 survey, 'What a Waste', by the Australia Institute found that Australian households throw out more than $5 billion worth of food each year. Fruit and vegetables are thrown out more than any other food type – $1.1 billion per year. We also throw out $872.5 million worth of fresh fish, poultry and meat, and $241 million of frozen food.

In addition to the waste of money, there are environmental costs caused by the greenhouse gases produced from the rotting food, from its transport, production and delivery, and from its huge amount of packaging. These all demonstrate the magnitude of the problem of our wasteful food habits.

Given all these factors, not to mention the potential financial savings to our households, perhaps we should think again about what to do with our leftovers that currently are finding their way to the garbage bin. Some people may shy away from the mere reheating of food to serve another day – after all, we would hardly want to get into a habit such as that expressed by Calvin Trillin, 'For thirty years my mother served the family nothing but leftovers. The original meal has never been found.' However, using up leftovers has many advantages.

I have always been an overestimator of the amount of food a family or guests can eat and invariably have had leftovers to use up. Even with six children, I regularly ended up with containers of food that were perfectly edible and correctly stored, but still eventually were thrown into the bin.

Now serving leftovers to children can be very challenging as they are spotted in an instant and are immediately rejected. With my grandmother's words coming back to haunt me about appreciating the value of food, I decided to develop new meals that incorporated the leftovers but gave them a new life of their own. By extension I vowed never again to throw out those remnants of tomato paste and jam, and to make good use of the bits and pieces of vegetables in the fridge.

I found it was remarkably easy once I set my mind to it. Even better, it made a significant improvement to the household budget. These recipes, developed over the past 30 years, are now put together in *Leftover Makeovers*. I hope they will prove useful and inspirational, as they can be adapted depending on your own style of cooking and what you have on hand. They will result in significant financial savings as well as contribute to the overall reduction of household food wastage.

Points to Remember

When storing leftovers, make sure that they are placed in small containers to cool down as quickly as possible.

Where appropriate, separate different food types into different containers.

Label and date the leftovers. Use refrigerated within 3 days. If they are not to be used within this time, freeze immediately.

Place leftovers in the fridge as soon as they are cool (hot food can interfere with the proper working of the fridge).

When leftovers are placed in the fridge, make sure there is space around the containers so their temperature drops quickly.

Leftovers can also be frozen in small containers. Use within one month.

Bring soups, gravies and casserole dishes to the boil then simmer for at least 2 to 3 minutes.

When reheating a leftover meal in the oven, the temperature should be set to 170°C.

Slow cookers are not recommended for reheating leftovers as they take too much time to come up to temperature.

To reheat a meal in the microwave, the food should be covered with a lid or cling wrap. Standing time should be allowed after the food is removed from the microwave. This method of reheating leftover food is better kept to small amounts, such as a single meal.

In this book, if a recipe states an oven temperature, it is for a fan forced oven. If your oven is not fan forced or fan assisted, increase the temperature by 20°C.

BREAD & BREADCRUMBS

One of the most useful of leftovers is bread. I hate seeing it sit in the packet going mouldy. It is easy to freeze, either in slices or processed to breadcrumbs for later use in recipes.

In some of the following recipes you are directed to remove the crusts from the slices of bread, in which case don't throw away the crusts but turn them into breadcrumbs to use in recipes such as Meatballs in Saucy Gravy (page 7), Brown Bread Ice Cream (page 21), Chicken and Vegetable Studel (page 236), Apple Strudel (page 238).

CHICKABOTIE

Serves 4

2 slices white bread
1 cup milk
2 tablespoons oil
600g minced chicken
1 onion, finely diced
2 teaspoons curry powder
1 tablespoon vinegar, any type
1 tablespoon chutney, any sort
2 tablespoons lemon juice
1 teaspoon salt
½ cup finely diced dried apricots
¼ cup chicken stock or water
½ cup chopped almonds or pine nuts
2 eggs

Break up the bread and place in a bowl with the milk and leave to stand for at least 5 minutes.

Heat the oil in a frying pan over medium-high heat and cook the chicken mince and onion until the mince is coloured and well broken up, stirring often.

Add the curry powder and cook for 1 minute. Add the vinegar, chutney, lemon juice, salt, apricots, stock and nuts. Mix well. Remove from the heat.

Squeeze the milk from the bread, reserving the milk, and add the bread to the mince mixture and mix well. Spoon into a casserole dish. Whisk the eggs with the milk from the bread and pour over the top. Bake for 30 minutes, or until set.

MEATBALLS IN SAUCY GRAVY

Serves 4

This meat mixture can be made into 16–20 meatballs or into 8 meat patties (rissoles).

500g minced beef
1 onion, grated
1 egg, lightly whisked
1 tablespoon tomato sauce (ketchup)
3 teaspoons chutney, any sort
2 teaspoons Worcestershire sauce
2 teaspoons soy sauce
½ teaspoon salt
1 cup fresh breadcrumbs (equivalent to 2 slices of bread)
2 tablespoons olive oil

Gravy
1¼ cups vegetable or chicken stock
2 teaspoons tomato sauce
2 teaspoons soy sauce
2 teaspoons sweet chilli sauce
2 teaspoons cornflour mixed to a paste with 2 tablespoons of
    cold water

In a large bowl, combine the mince, onion, egg, tomato sauce, chutney, Worcestershire sauce, soy sauce, salt and breadcrumbs. Mix well then using wet hands shape the mixture into 16–20 meatballs or 8 patties.

Heat the oil in a frying pan over medium-high heat and cook for 3 minutes on one side, then turn and cook for a further 3 minutes, or until the meatballs or patties are cooked through. Remove from the pan and keep warm.

To make the gravy, discard any fat from the pan, pour in the stock, tomato sauce, soy sauce and sweet chilli sauce and bring to the boil, stirring. To thicken stir in some or all of the cornflour paste. Add salt and pepper to taste.

Return the meatballs or patties to the pan and turn to coat with the gravy.

Serve with creamy mashed potato and seasonal vegetables.

SAUSAGE ROLLS

Makes 20—24

300g sausage mince
300g minced beef
1 onion, grated
½ carrot, grated
½ cup fresh breadcrumbs (wholemeal preferably,
   equivalent to 1 wholemeal slice)
2 tablespoons ricotta (optional)
1 dessertspoon chutney, relish or tomato sauce
2 teaspoons soy sauce
2 teaspoons Worcestershire sauce
2 sheets frozen puff pastry, thawed

Heat the oven to 200°C. Line 2 baking trays with baking paper.

Combine all the ingredients, except for the pastry, and mix well.

Cut each pastry sheet in two equal pieces and brush down one long edge
of each piece with water.

Divide the sausage meat mixture into 4 portions. Form each one into a long
sausage and place one lengthways on each piece of pastry.

Roll up and cut into 5 or 6 pieces. Prick each one twice with a fork.

Place on baking trays and bake for 15 minutes, or until the pastry is well
puffed and golden and the meat cooked through.

BOBOTIE

Serves 4–6

2 slices white bread
1 cup milk
2 tablespoons olive oil
750g good quality minced beef
1 onion, finely diced
2 teaspoons curry powder
1 tablespoon brown sugar
1 tablespoon vinegar, any type
1 tablespoon chutney, any type
½ cup slivered almonds
½ teaspoon finely grated lemon rind
1 tablespoon lemon juice
2 eggs
¾ teaspoon salt

Heat the oven to 170°C. Grease a 20cm casserole or baking dish.

Break up the bread a little and pour the milk over it. Leave to stand for a few minutes.

Heat the oil in a frying pan and sauté the meat and onion until the beef changes colour, add the curry powder and cook for 1 minute more. Turn down the heat and add the brown sugar, vinegar, chutney, almonds, lemon rind and lemon juice. Squeeze the bread (reserving the milk) and add to the meat mixture. Cook for 1 minute more. Spoon into the prepared casserole dish.

Beat the eggs and salt with the milk from the bread and pour evenly over the meat mixture.

Bake for 35 minutes, or until the mixture is set.

CHEESE AND CAPSICUM CHARLOTTE

Serves 4–6

6 slices bread, thin cut
75g butter or substitute
¾ cup milk
1 tablespoon olive oil
125g roasted red capsicum
1 leek, white part only, or 1 onion, finely diced
1 cup chopped mushrooms
3 eggs, separated
1½ tablespoons flour
125g grated cheese
pinch of nutmeg
½ teaspoon salt
pinch of white pepper
½ cup cream or milk

Heat the oven to 170°C. Grease a 20cm pie or casserole dish.

Cut off and discard the crusts of 4 slices of bread. Spread with 30g of the butter. Cut each slice into 4 triangles and line the prepared dish, butter side out.

Tear the other 2 slices of bread into cubes and pour the milk over. Leave to stand for 10 minutes.

Meanwhile, heat the oil in a frying pan over medium heat and sauté the capsicum, leek and mushrooms for 5 minutes, stirring often.

In a bowl soften the remaining butter, add the egg yolks and whisk until well incorporated. Mix in the flour, soaked bread, cheese, nutmeg, salt, pepper and cream and whisk until smooth. Stir in the vegetables.

Beat the egg whites until stiff and mix through the vegetable mixture. Pour into the prepared dish and bake for 35–40 minutes, or until set.

MINI BRUSCHETTAS

These crispy little treats have a range of uses. Our children used to love them spread with butter and Vegemite, peanut butter or cheese spread (page 116).

They can be used as a canapé topped with some of the suggestions that follow the recipe.

slices of sandwich bread

Heat the oven to 120°C. Grease or line baking trays with baking paper.

Remove the crusts from the bread and cut 4 rounds from each slice. Spray with olive oil or brush with a little melted butter.

Place on the prepared oven trays and bake for about 20 minutes, or until crisp. Store in an airtight container.

Toppings

- Finely diced deseeded tomatoes, mixed with fresh herbs and a little lemon juice and olive oil.

- Cream cheese mixed with a little lemon juice and chopped capers. Pipe or spoon onto mini bruschettas and top with a small piece of smoked salmon, trout or smoked chicken.

- Thin slices of roasted beef with horseradish cream and a small piece of semi-dried tomato.

SAVOURY BREAD CASES

Each slice of bread makes one savoury case. These cases keep well in an airtight container. If your bread is stale, it may not be pliable enough to press into the muffin tins. If this is the case, heat each bread slice for a few seconds in the microwave. This will soften it and you will be able to easily press into place. The bread cases can be filled as required for a quick snack or canapés as needed. Several suggested fillings follow.

slices of square sandwich bread

Heat the oven to 150°C. Grease as many ½ cup capacity muffin holes as you have slices of bread.

Remove the crusts from the bread. If desired, brush with a little melted butter, or spray with cooking oil, but it is by no means necessary. Bake for 10–15 minutes, or until dry and light golden.

Filling: basic sauce recipe (about 2 cups)
60g butter
2 tablespoons flour
1½ cups milk
¼ cup cream or sour cream
½ teaspoon Dijon mustard

In a saucepan melt the butter over a low heat, then add the flour and cook for 1 minute while stirring. Gradually add the milk, while whisking constantly, and bring to the boil. Simmer for 2 minutes. Add the cream, mustard and salt and pepper to taste.

Add any of the following ingredients to this basic mixture:

> ½–¾ cup smoked salmon, 1 chopped hardboiled egg and
>   ½ cup grated cheese
> 1 cup chopped cooked asparagus and ½ cup grated cheese
> 2 finely sliced spring onions, 125g diced cooked bacon or
>   ham and ½ cup corn kernels

Antipasto Tarts

½ cup sliced Kalamata olives
½ cup diced roasted capsicum
¼ cup diced deseeded tomatoes
⅓ cup diced feta
2 tablespoons chopped basil
2 teaspoons olive oil
1 teaspoon lemon juice

Combine all the ingredients. Just before serving, spoon the mixture into the bread cases and top with some shaved parmesan cheese. Serve immediately.

WELSH RAREBIT

Serves 2—4

This old favourite has stood the test of time. It can still often be found at 'bring-a-plate' functions, at least in country areas. It is very tasty served either hot or cold.

> 2 slices lean bacon, rind removed and finely diced
> 1 small onion, grated
> 1 cup grated tasty cheese
> 1 egg, lightly whisked
> 1 tablespoon chopped parsley
> 2 teaspoons tomato sauce
> 2 teaspoons Worcestershire sauce
> **4 slices bread**

In a bowl mix together the bacon, onion, cheese, egg, parsley, tomato sauce and Worcestershire sauce.

Toast the bread under the grill on one side. Turn the bread over and spread generously with the topping and place under the grill until it is melted and bubbly.

Cut each slice into 4 triangles and serve hot with soup. They can also be served cold. Store in an airtight container in the fridge.

CRUMBED STUFFED MUSHROOMS

Serves 2

This recipe can easily be doubled to provide an ample entrée for 4. Serve with a little sweet chilli sauce.

45g cream cheese
¼ teaspoon chopped fresh thyme
1 tablespoon grated tasty cheese
1 teaspoon lemon juice
pinch of paprika
pinch of salt
250g button mushrooms
½ cup (approximately) plain flour
1 egg
**1 cup (approximately) fresh breadcrumbs (equivalant to
    about 2 slices of bread)**
canola oil for deep frying

In a bowl cream together the cream cheese, thyme, tasty cheese, lemon juice, paprika and salt.

Remove the stalks from the mushrooms and fill the cavities with the cheese mixture.

Roll the filled mushrooms first in the flour, then the egg, and finally the breadcrumbs, pressing the coating on firmly. Place in a single layer on a tray and refrigerate for at least 30 minutes.

Heat the oil over medium-high heat to approximately 180°C and place the mushrooms a few at a time into the hot oil, cap side down. Cook for 2 minutes, then turn and cook the underside until the coating is crisp.

Drain on crumpled paper towel.

FRENCH TOAST

Serves 4

2 eggs
½ cup milk
4 thick slices stale bread

In a bowl whisk the eggs and milk together. Quickly dip the bread into the mixture then cook in a non-stick pan or shallow fry until golden brown on each side. Serve with crispy bacon and sautéed tomatoes and mushrooms for breakfast, or for a sweet treat drizzled with maple syrup, honey or golden syrup.

CROUTONS

Makes about 16

Croutons are an excellent stand-by as a crispy garnish for soup. Store in an airtight container, where they will keep for weeks. They can also be later crushed and used as a coating for fish or chicken.

4 slices stale bread, crust removed
olive oil cooking spray

Heat the oven to 100°C. Line 2 baking trays with baking paper or grease.

Cut the bread into small cubes and spray lightly on both sides with the olive oil. Place on the trays and bake until crisp and golden.

MELBA TOASTS

Our children used to have these as an after-school snack, spread with butter and Vegemite or peanut butter or topped with sliced tomato.

leftover sliced bread (any sort), crusts removed

Heat the oven to 100°C. Line 2 baking trays with baking paper or grease.

Diagonally cut each slice in half and place the triangles on the trays. Bake for 30–40 minutes, or until crisp and golden. Store in an airtight container, where they will keep, if dried out properly, for weeks.

Like croutons, these can also later be crushed to make a crumb coating for fish or chicken.

APPLE AND BLUEBERRY CHARLOTTE

Serves 4—6

This pudding is a twist on an old-fashioned favourite and is absolutely delicious. If you don't have blueberries, just use the apple. In my opinion, the bread crust is as delicious as any pastry.

> 5 cooking apples, such as Granny Smiths
> ½ cup water
> ¼ cup (approximately) sugar
> ½–¾ cup fresh or frozen blueberries
> **6–7 slices sandwich bread, crusts removed**
> 125g butter, melted

Heat the oven to 170°C. Grease a 20cm casserole dish.

Peel and core the apples, then cut into large cubes. Place in a saucepan with the water and cook until the apples are soft and mushy. Stir in the sugar, and finally the blueberries. Test for sweetness and add extra sugar if necessary.

Cut each slice of bread into 3 strips. Dip each strip quickly into the butter and line the dish, including the sides, in a single layer. Set aside any remaining strips.

Pour in the apple and blueberry mixture. Top with the last of the bread strips.

Bake for 30–40 minutes, or until the bread is crisp and golden.

Serve with vanilla ice cream, mascarpone or yoghurt.

APPLE BROWN BETTY

Serves 4–6

1kg cooking apples (such as Granny Smiths)
1 tablespoon lemon juice
2–3 tablespoons sugar
4 slices stale bread, crusts removed
½ cup brown sugar, firmly packed
½ teaspoon ground cinnamon
¼ teaspoon ground nutmeg
pinch of ground cloves
125g butter, melted

Heat the oven to 160°C. Grease a 20cm casserole dish.

Peel and core the apples, then cut each apple into 8 pieces. Place in the prepared casserole dish and mix in the lemon juice and sugar.

Stack the bread slices on a board and cut into 16 squares by cutting crossways then lengthways. Place the bread squares into a bowl and mix with the brown sugar, cinnamon, nutmeg, cloves and melted butter. Spread evenly over the top of the apple and bake for 30 minutes, or until the topping is crisp and golden and the apples are tender.

Serve with vanilla ice cream.

BROWN BREAD ICE CREAM

Makes about 450ml

This ice cream has a delicious cinnamon crunch.

>   4 egg whites
>   1 cup icing sugar
>   4 egg yolks
>   2 teaspoons golden syrup
>   ½ teaspoon vanilla extract or essence
>   1¼ cups pouring cream
>   30g butter
>   **1 cup brown breadcrumbs (equivalent to 2 slices of**
>   **wholemeal bread)**
>   ½ cup raw sugar
>   ½ teaspoon ground cinnamon

In a bowl beat the egg whites until stiff peaks form, add the icing sugar and beat until stiff peaks form once more.

In another bowl, whisk the egg yolks, golden syrup and vanilla together until well combined, and then beat into the egg white mixture.

Whip the cream until soft peaks form and fold into the egg yolk mixture. Pour into a 2-litre ice cream container or ice cream trays, cover the surface with cling wrap and place in the freezer. Leave until half frozen.

Meanwhile, melt the butter in a frying pan over medium-low heat and sauté the breadcrumbs for 4 minutes, stirring. Add the raw sugar and cinnamon and cook, stirring, until breadcrumbs are crisp. Cool completely.

Remove the ice cream from the freezer, fold through the breadcrumbs and return to the freezer to freeze completely.

Remove the ice cream from the freezer for a few minutes before serving to allow it to soften slightly.

PEAR AND RAISIN PUDDING

Serves 6

The best word I can think of to describe this loaf is 'squidgy' – it is designed for those who love a very moist cake, and is delicious served as a pudding or even sliced when cold and spread with butter. It actually reminds me of a treat my father used to enjoy every Sunday evening. In those days before the advent of sliced bread, each week the thick crust ends of the bread would be saved for Sunday night tea. Dad would soak them in milk, drain off the excess liquid, then toast them under the grill. When they came out, he spread them with literally lashings of butter. I have to say it tasted so good but pretty disastrous for the waistline or cholesterol level of course. However, it is totally worth trying just for the taste experience.

250g bread, either slices or whole
1 egg
90g sugar
¾ cup milk
2 tablespoons lemon juice
grated rind 1 lemon
½ cup plain flour
2 teaspoons baking powder
1 teaspoon ground nutmeg
2 pears, peeled, cored and diced
1 cup raisins
2 teaspoons melted butter
2 teaspoons sugar, extra
½ teaspoon ground cinnamon

Tear up the bread and place in a bowl, cover with water and leave to stand for 30 minutes. Place a tea towel in a colander and pour the bread mixture into this. Draw the edges of the tea towel together and squeeze to remove as much liquid as possible.

Heat the oven to 150°C. Grease a square 20cm tin and line the base with baking paper, then grease again.

In a bowl whisk the egg and sugar together. In another bowl mix the milk and lemon juice and allow to stand for 1 minute, then add to the egg mixture, together with the lemon rind, flour, baking powder, nutmeg and soaked bread. Mix well until smooth, then fold in the pears and raisins.

Spoon into the prepared tin, smoothing out the top, and bake for 1½ hours. Remove from the oven, allow to stand in the tin for 10 minutes, then turn out onto a wire rack. Brush the top with the melted butter, sprinkle with the extra sugar and cinnamon.

SCOTCH BUN WITH SPICE ICING

Serves 12

This recipe came from one of my late aunts. Without the icing, it is very nice served with Egg Yolk Custard (page 144) and ice cream. However, as a cake with my Nan's special nutmeg icing, it is a real treat.

Pastry
60g butter
½ cup sugar
1 egg
½ teaspoon bicarbonate of soda
½ cup self-raising flour
1 cup plain flour
2 teaspoons milk

Filling
1½ cups warm water
10 slices stale white bread
1½ teaspoons mixed spice
½ teaspoon ground cinnamon
½ teaspoon ground nutmeg
1 tablespoon cocoa powder
½ cup brown sugar
3 teaspoons self-raising flour
grated rind ½ lemon
2 eggs, lightly beaten

Icing

1½ cups icing sugar
90g butter, softened
¾ teaspoon ground nutmeg
¼ teaspoon vanilla extract or essence
1 tablespoon (approximately) boiling water

To make the pastry, cream the butter and sugar in a bowl, then whisk in the egg. Fold in the sifted bicarbonate of soda and flours together with the milk. Wrap in cling wrap and place in fridge while preparing the filling.

To make the filling, pour the water over the bread and allow to stand for 5 minutes, then whisk until it forms a paste. Add the spices, cocoa, sugar, flour, lemon rind and eggs and mix well.

Heat the oven to 160°C. Grease a 20cm square cake tin.

Cut the pastry in half and roll out each half to fit the size of the tin. Line the base of the tin with one half of the pastry. Spoon over the filling. Cover the top with the other half of pastry. Prick the pastry in several places with a fork. Bake for 30 minutes, or until the pastry is crisp and golden and the filling is set. Allow to cool in the tin. Ice when completely cold.

To make the icing, mix together the icing sugar, butter, nutmeg and vanilla with enough boiling water to make a smooth spreadable consistency.

Treacle Tart

Serves 6–8

Pastry
60g butter
60g sugar
1 egg yolk
125g plain flour
1 teaspoon baking powder

Filling
300g golden syrup
150ml pouring or thickened cream
1 egg, lightly whisked
85g (1½ cups) fresh white breadcrumbs
60g ground almonds
2 teaspoons lemon juice

To make the pastry, cream the butter and sugar together in a bowl until light and fluffy, then whisk in the egg yolk. In another bowl, mix the flour and baking powder together then fold into the butter mixture. Gently mix until it comes together. Wrap in cling wrap and place in fridge for 30 minutes before rolling.

Grease a 2.5cm deep 20cm round pie dish.

Sprinkle a workbench or board with a little flour. Remove the pastry from the fridge and sprinkle with a little extra flour. Roll out to fit the pie dish, including the sides, and line the prepared dish. Trim excess, wrap in cling wrap and store in the fridge for later use.

Heat the oven to 180°C.

To make the filling, heat the golden syrup in a saucepan over a low heat until melted. Whisk in the cream, and then the egg. Fold in the breadcrumbs, ground almonds and lemon juice.

Cool for 15 minutes then pour into the pastry case. Place in the oven and bake for 10 minutes, then reduce the heat to 160°C and bake for 20 minutes more, or until the filling is set.

Serve with whipped cream or mascarpone.

PULLED BREAD

Serves 6—8

Pulled bread is an excellent accompaniment to soup and is a good way to use up stale unsliced bread.

½–1 loaf of unsliced bread
½ cup (approximately) milk

Heat the oven to 170°C. Grease 2 baking trays or line with baking paper.

Cut bread in half and pull approximately ¼ cup-sized pieces from the inside of the loaf. Brush with just a little milk.

Place on trays and bake for 10 minutes, or until crisp and golden.

Store in an airtight container.

CEREAL, NUTS, PASTA & RICE

Invariably in our house small amounts of cereal would accumulate in the bottom of packets as cereal preferences of the children changed from week to week. The recipes in this section provide some examples of what can be done to use them up, if this should be an issue in your household also. Smaller amounts can be added to commercial or home-made muesli (see recipe page 255) but there are numerous other ways to utilise them, such as in biscuits and slices and, as in the case of cornflakes, as a crunchy topping for sweet or savoury casserole dishes.

It is good to use up leftover nuts quite quickly as they have the potential to go rancid with storing. Small amounts of leftover nuts can be added to muesli or used in biscuit dough. When crumbing bread for coatings, add any leftover nuts (crushed) to the mix for extra flavour and texture. Crumble toppings for fruit are also enhanced by the inclusion of about one tablespoon of very finely chopped nuts.

Leftover cooked pasta is very versatile and can be used up in salads and casserole type dishes. It can be added to a simple pasta sauce, topped with cheese and baked in a moderate oven for about 25 minutes until bubbling. Served with garlic bread and salad, it makes an entirely new meal. If you are making cauliflower cheese, add some leftover pasta for extra texture. Of course when added to a well-flavoured cheese sauce it makes delicious macaroni cheese, made all the more so by the addition of cooked, smoked or even drained, tinned fish or cooked diced vegetables.

Cooked rice should be refrigerated quickly and used within two days. Make sure that you thoroughly heat it through when re-using. Add to savoury pie fillings or turn into savoury dishes such as Fried Rice (see recipe page 58) or in rice puddings. It also makes a good addition to sweet or savoury pancakes, which are very well received by children (see recipe page 57). Try layering cooked rice with a flavoursome pasta sauce, finishing with the sauce, sprinkle with grated tasty and parmesan cheese and bake for 30 minutes in a moderate oven.

CEREAL

Cornflakes

(See also: Creamy Seafood Mornay variation, page 74;
Tuna Mornay variation, page 151; Potato Crisp, page 171;
Honey and Cornflake Dreams, page 272; Apple Crisp, page 273.)

CRISPY FISH TART

Serves 6—8

This tasty tart is an unusual way to use up leftover cornflakes and is also handy for using up cooked fish fillets. It is nice served warm or cold.

Pastry
1 cup plain flour
½ cup self-raising flour
½ teaspoon salt
90g butter
1 tablespoon lemon juice
¼ cup (approximately) cold water

Filling
2 eggs
1 cup milk
1 tablespoon lemon juice
425g tin tuna in brine or spring water, drained and flaked
    (or **300g flaked cooked fish**)
1 tablespoon finely chopped parsley

2 spring onions, finely sliced
1 small onion, grated
½ teaspoon Dijon mustard
2 teaspoons mayonnaise
1 teaspoon Worcestershire sauce
60g tasty cheese, grated

Topping
1¼ cups (approximately) cornflakes,
 crumbed but not too fine
70g tasty cheese, finely grated
½ teaspoon curry powder
¼ teaspoon sweet paprika

Heat the oven to 200°C. Grease an 18cm x 28cm lasagne dish.

In a bowl combine the flours and salt and rub in the butter with your fingertips until the mixture resembles fine breadcrumbs, or alternatively, process to this stage in a food processor then transfer to a bowl.

Mix in the lemon juice and cold water until the mixture forms a soft dough. You may need to add a little extra water if the dough is too dry. Line the prepared dish by pressing out the dough to an even thickness.

To make the filling, whisk the eggs, milk and lemon juice together in a large bowl, then fold in the rest of the ingredients until well combined. Pour over the pastry.

To make the topping, combine all ingredients and sprinkle over filling.

Bake for 10 minutes, then reduce heat to 160°C and bake a further 20–25 minutes, or until the filling is set. Allow to stand in the dish for a few minutes before cutting into squares with a sharp knife to serve.

Serve with fresh seasonal vegetables or green salad.

CHOCOLATE CORNFLAKE COOKIES

Makes about 28

210g butter
90g sugar
180g plain flour
1 teaspoon baking powder
30g cocoa powder
1 cup cornflakes

Icing (optional)
1½ cups icing sugar
1 tablespoon cocoa powder
1 dessertspoon softened butter
boiling water

Heat the oven to 160°C. Line 3 baking trays with baking paper.

In a large bowl, cream the butter and sugar until the mixture is light and fluffy, then mix in the flour, baking powder, cocoa and cornflakes until combined. Place heaped teaspoonfuls of the mixture on the trays and bake for 15 minutes. Remove from oven and leave to cool on the trays for 8–10 minutes, then remove from the trays and cool completely on a wire rack, and ice with chocolate icing if desired.

To make the icing sift the icing sugar and cocoa together into a bowl and add the butter. Stir in the boiling water, 1 teaspoon at a time, until the mixture becomes a smooth spreadable icing (not too thick).

Store in an airtight container.

Muesli

MUESLI CRISPS

Makes about 30

90g butter
100g brown sugar
100g caster sugar
2 eggs
¾ cup muesli
¼ chopped dried apricots
½ cup desiccated coconut
1¼ cups self-raising flour

Heat the oven to 150°C. Line 3 baking trays with baking paper.

In a large bowl, cream the butter and sugars together until light and fluffy, then whisk in the eggs until well combined. Fold in the muesli, apricots, coconut and flour, and mix well.

Drop teaspoonfuls of the mixture onto the trays about 3.5cm apart to allow room for spreading.

Bake for 15 minutes, or until golden brown. Leave on the trays for 5 minutes, then remove to a wire rack to cool completely.

Store in an airtight container.

Wheat Biscuits

◆

WHEATY MEAT LOAF

Serves 4–6

750g best minced beef
1 large onion, grated
2 breakfast wheat biscuits, crushed
½ cup milk
1 egg, lightly whisked
1 small carrot, peeled and finely grated
1 small zucchini, grated
1 egg, lightly whisked
3 teaspoons soy sauce
2 teaspoons chutney
2 teaspoons tomato sauce (ketchup)
2 teaspoons Worcestershire sauce
1 teaspoon salt

Mix together all the ingredients in a large bowl and leave to stand for 30 minutes in the fridge.

Heat the oven to 190°C. Grease a 14cm x 25cm (approximately) loaf tin.

Spoon the mixture evenly into the prepared tin. Bake for 10 minutes, then reduce heat to 160°C and bake for 30–40 minutes more, or until golden and cooked through.

Allow to stand in the tin for 10 minutes before removing to a platter.

Cut into 1cm slices and serve with tomato sauce or chutney and seasonal vegetables.

CHEWY CHOCOLATE SLICE

Makes 16–20 squares

This fruity chocolate slice has a crunchiness softened by the chewiness of
the sultanas contained in it. It makes good use of the last couple of wheat
biscuits in a packet and was always a great favourite with our children.
The chocolate icing is optional, but adds a nice glaze and a little extra
sweetness.

> 1 cup plain flour
> 1 teaspoon baking powder
> ½ cup sugar
> 1½ tablespoons cocoa powder
> **2 breakfast wheat biscuits, crushed to the point of flakes**
> ½ cup sultanas
> ½ teaspoon vanilla extract or essence
> 150g butter, melted
>
> **Icing (optional)**
> 1½ cups icing sugar
> 3 teaspoons cocoa powder
> 2 teaspoons butter, softened
> 1 tablespoon (approximately) boiling water

Heat the oven to 160°C. Grease an 18cm x 28cm lamington tin.

In a bowl mix together the flour, baking powder, sugar, cocoa, biscuits,
sultanas, vanilla and butter until well combined. Place in the prepared tin
and press down evenly. Bake for 25 minutes, or until cooked through.

While the slice is cooking, prepare the icing as follows. Mix together the
icing sugar and cocoa. Add the softened butter and enough boiling water to
make a spreadable icing consistency.

When the slice is removed from the oven, immediately pour over the icing and spread evenly. Mark the slice into 16–20 squares with a sharp knife, then leave to cool in the tin.

When cold, cut the slice along the marked lines.

Store in an airtight container.

Rolled oats

(See also Chewy Muesli Cookies, page 44.)

As winter comes to an end, even the most avid porridge lovers will most likely move on to a lighter cereal over the summer months. This can leave the pantry with leftover rolled oats languishing in the packet and taking up valuable cupboard space. However, there are quite a number of ways they can be used up. For example, leftover dry oats can be added to meatballs, rissoles or meat loaves – add about I tablespoon per 600g meat. Add I tablespoon of quick oats to a stew or casserole to help thicken the gravy as it cooks. Leftover cooked porridge can be added to bread mixtures as can dry rolled oats. There are many recipes that can incorporate rolled oats also, here are a few.

◆

COFFEE DATE CAKE

Serves 8

This deliciously moist cake is wonderful served with tea or coffee, but un-iced could serve well as a dessert with whipped cream or mascarpone.

2 teaspoons instant coffee dissolved in 1 cup of boiling water*
1 cup chopped dates
½ teaspoon bicarbonate of soda
125g butter
1 cup sugar
2 eggs, lightly beaten
1 cup plain flour
1 teaspoon baking powder

¼ teaspoon ground nutmeg
½ cup rolled oats
¾ cup chopped walnuts or hazelnuts

Icing
1½ cups icing sugar, sifted
2 teaspoons butter, softened
2 teaspoons coffe powder or granules dissolved in
     3 teaspoons of boiling water
extra boiling water

Mix together the hot coffee mixture, dates and bicarbonate of soda, and set aside to cool.

Heat the oven to 150°C. Grease a 20cm round cake tin and line the base with baking paper, then grease again.

In a bowl cream the butter and sugar until light and fluffy, then whisk in the eggs. In another bowl combine the flour, baking powder, nutmeg and rolled oats, then with a metal spoon fold into the cooled date mixture with ½ cup of the nuts.

Pour the mixture into the prepared tin and smooth out the surface. Bake for 40–50 minutes, or until a metal skewer inserted into the centre comes out clean. Turn out onto a wire rack to cool completely.

To make the icing, placing the icing sugar in a bowl. Mix in the butter and coffee mixture, adding a little extra boiling water (very gradually) if needed. Ice the top of the cake and sprinkle immediately with the remaining ¼ cup of chopped nuts.

* *Leftover brewed coffee, reheated to boiling point, can be used instead of the combined instant coffee and boiling water.*

APPLE CRUMBLE

Serves 4–6

3–4 cups stewed apple, sweetened to taste*
¼ cup rolled oats
½ cup self-raising flour
¼ cup brown sugar, firmly packed
60g butter

Heat the oven to 170°C. Grease a 20cm casserole or pie dish.

Place the apple in the prepared casserole or pie dish.

Place oats, flour and brown sugar in a bowl, add the butter and rub it into the dry ingredients with the fingertips until the mixture resembles breadcrumbs. Alternatively, use a food processor for this. Spread the mixture evenly over the apple.

Bake for 30 minutes, or until topping is golden brown.

Serve with vanilla ice cream or Egg Yolk Custard (page 144).

* *To make stewed apple, peel, core and slice 1kg of cooking apples. Place in a saucepan with ¼ cup water and heat until just boiling, then reduce heat and simmer while stirring frequently for 15 minutes, or until the apples are soft. Add sugar to taste. The apple mixture can be used in this recipe, hot or cold.*

CARROT AND APPLE MUFFINS

Makes about 18

1/3 cup honey
2 eggs
1 cup milk or plain yoghurt
1 tablespoon lemon juice
1 cup self-raising flour
1 cup wholemeal self-raising flour
1 teaspoon baking powder
2 teaspoons ground cinnamon
1 cup quick oats*
1 cup grated carrot
1 apple, cored and grated
½ cup sultanas

Heat the oven to 180°C. Grease 18 x ¼-cup capacity muffin tins.

In a large bowl, whisk together the honey, eggs, milk or yoghurt and lemon juice. In another bowl, combine the flours, baking powder, cinnamon and oats, and fold into the wet mixture, together with the carrot, apple and sultanas. Spoon into the prepared muffin tins until two-thirds full.

Bake for 20–25 minutes, or until a skewer inserted into the centre comes out clean.

Allow to stand in the tins for 5 minutes, then turn out onto a wire rack to cool completely.

* *If you only have rolled oats, not quick oats, simply process the rolled oats to a finer texture in a food processor.*

NUTTY-OATIES

Makes about 24

125g peanut butter (smooth or crunchy)
125g butter
1 cup sugar
1 egg
1 cup self-raising flour
½ cup rolled oats
¼ cup chopped nuts (any sort), optional

Heat the oven to 150°C. Grease 3 x 30cm baking trays or line with baking paper.

In a bowl cream the peanut butter, butter and sugar together until light and fluffy. Whisk in the egg, then fold in the flour, oats and nuts (if using).

Roll heaped teaspoonfuls of mixture into balls and place 8 on each tray, evenly spaced. Press down slightly with a fork that has been dipped in flour.

Bake for 12–15 minutes, or until light golden brown. Remove to wire racks to cool.

HONEY AND OAT BREAD

Makes 1 large loaf or 12 bread rolls

This loaf keeps fresher longer than the usual homemade bread.

 3½ cups plain flour
 ½ cup rolled oats
 4 teaspoons dried yeast
 2 teaspoons salt
 1½ teaspoons honey
 1 egg, lightly beaten
 1 tablespoon olive or light olive oil
 1½ cups (approximately) warm water
 1 egg, lightly beaten, extra
 1–2 tablespoons rolled oats, extra

In a large bowl, mix together the flour, oats, yeast and salt. Make a well in the centre and pour in the honey, egg, oil and enough warm water to make a soft dough.

Place a tea towel over the bowl and leave to rise for about 50 minutes, or until approximately doubled in size.

Turn out onto a lightly floured board and knead for about 3 minutes until smooth. To make a loaf, cut the dough in half and shape each into a ball.

Grease a 13cm x 21cm (approximately) bread tin. Place the loaves side by side in the tin, then cover with a tea towel and leave them to rise almost to the top of the tin.

Meanwhile, heat the oven to 200°C.

Brush gently with the extra beaten egg and sprinkle with the extra oats. Bake at 200°C for 15 minutes, then reduce the temperature to 180°C and bake for 25 minutes more, or until the loaf sounds hollow when tapped with a fingernail. Turn out onto a wire rack to cool.

To make bread rolls, line a 30cm x 30cm baking tray with baking paper.

Cut the dough into 12 equal portions and knead each into a ball. Place evenly on the prepared tray. Leave the rolls to rise for 15–20 minutes until approximately doubled in size, then brush carefully with the extra beaten egg and sprinkle with the extra oats. Bake at 200°C for 15–20 minutes, or until the rolls are golden brown.

Puffed rice cereal

◆

CHEWY MUESLI COOKIES

Makes about 24

60g butter
½ cup brown sugar, lightly packed
¼ cup golden syrup
¼ cup honey
1 teaspoon finely grated orange rind
1 cup puffed rice cereal
¼ cup desiccated coconut
½ cup rolled oats
1 cup self-raising flour
1 cup sultanas
½ cup diced dried apricots
¾ cup small choc dots
¼ cup chopped hazelnuts (optional)
¼ cup sesame seeds
½ teaspoon bicarbonate of soda
1 tablespoon boiling water

Heat the oven to 160°C. Grease 4 baking trays or line with baking paper.

Place the butter, brown sugar, golden syrup and honey in a small saucepan and melt over a low heat. Remove and cool for 5 minutes.

In a large bowl, mix together the orange rind, puffed rice, coconut, oats, flour, sultanas, apricots, choc dots, hazelnuts and sesame seeds.

In a cup mix the bicarbonate of soda with the boiling water until dissolved.

Pour the butter and bicarbonate of soda mixtures into the cereal mixture and stir until well combined. With slightly damp hands, roll dessertspoonfuls of the mixture into balls and place on the prepared trays about 4cm apart to allow room for spreading.

Bake for approximately 12 minutes, or until golden. Be careful that they do not burn.

Allow to stand on the trays for 5 minutes, then remove to a wire rack to cool completely.

BUBBLE CHOC CHEWS

Makes about 18

white of 1 large egg
½ cup caster sugar
1 teaspoon boiling water
¼ teaspoon vanilla extract or essence
⅓ cup small choc dots
½ cup desiccated coconut
1 cup puffed rice cereal

Heat the oven to 160°C. Line 2 baking trays with baking paper or grease.

Beat the egg white with the sugar and boiling water until stiff peaks form. Fold in the vanilla, choc chips, coconut and puffed rice.

Drop rounded teaspoonfuls of the mixture onto the prepared baking trays and bake for 12 minutes, or until light golden and crisp on the outside.

Transfer to wire racks to cool completely.

WHITE CHRISTMAS (WITHOUT COPHA)

Makes about 30 small pieces

Personally, I dislike the taste and texture of copha, so I haven't used it here. This version is richer and creamier than regular White Christmas slice. If preferred, it can be spooned and allowed to set in patty paper cases for individual serves.

> 375g white chocolate melts
> ½ cup cream
> 1 cup dried mixed fruit
> **1 cup puffed rice cereal**
> 1 cup desiccated coconut
> ½ cup skim or full-cream milk powder
> ¼ cup halved glacé cherries (optional)

Line an 18cm x 28cm tin with baking paper.

Melt the chocolate in a heatproof bowl over a saucepan of simmering water (do not let the base of the bowl touch the water). In a small saucepan boil the cream.

Mix the dried fruit, puffed rice, coconut and milk powder into the melted white chocolate. Stir in the cream and cherries and mix together carefully until well combined.

Press into the prepared tin and allow to set at room temperature, which will take about 1 hour. Cut into small squares with a knife dipped in boiling water.

Store in an airtight container in the fridge.

PEANUT BUTTER DELIGHTS

Makes about 12

2 rounded tablespoons peanut butter
30g butter
1 teaspoon honey
½ cup icing sugar
½ cup puffed rice cereal
1 cup desiccated coconut, extra

In a medium saucepan, melt the peanut butter, butter and honey over a low heat. Remove from heat, add the icing sugar, puffed rice and ¼ cup of the coconut and mix until combined.

Place the remaining coconut in a bowl.

Roll the peanut mixture into walnut-sized balls, coat with the coconut and place on a tray lined with baking paper for about 1 hour, or until set.

VARIATION

Instead of rolling the balls in coconut, simply place on trays to set. Roll in melted dark chocolate and place on baking paper to set once more.

NUTS

(See also: Nutty-Oaties, page 41; Muesli, page 255;
Tipsy Fruities, page 258.)

PEANUT BISCUITS

Makes about 24

125g peanut butter
125g softened butter
½ teaspoon vanilla extract or essence
200g sugar
1 egg
180g self-raising flour
½ **cup (approximately) chopped nuts**, peanuts are perhaps
   the best here, but any sort will do

Heat the oven to 160°C. Line 3 baking trays with baking paper.

In a large bowl, beat the peanut butter, butter, vanilla and sugar until creamy. Whisk in the egg, then fold in the flour and nuts and stir with a metal spoon until very well combined.

Roll teaspoonfuls of dough into balls and place on the trays, allowing a little room for spreading. Press down lightly with a fork.

Bake for 12–15 minutes, or until golden. Place on a wire rack to cool.

NAN PURTON'S SULTANA CAKE

Serves 12

This recipe originated from my grandmother's collection of recipes which she inherited from her parents' bakery. It is absolutely delicious – I've never tasted a sultana cake better.

> 500g sultanas
> 250g butter
> 250g sugar
> 3 eggs
> 375g plain flour
> 1 teaspoon baking powder
> grated rind 1 large lemon
> 1½ tablespoons boiling water
> **1–2 tablespoons almonds, whole or slivered**

Place the sultanas in a saucepan, cover with water, bring to the boil then simmer gently for 3 minutes. Strain off the liquid and discard. Cool the sultanas.

Heat the oven to 150°C. Grease a deep 20cm round tin and line the base with baking paper, then grease again.

Beat the butter and sugar in a large bowl until light and creamy, then add the eggs and beat well. Fold in the dry ingredients, lemon rind and sultanas until well mixed. Last, mix in the boiling water.

Pour into the prepared tin, smoothing out the top and leaving a very slight indent in the centre. Decorate the top with almonds.

Bake for 2–2½ hours, or until a metal skewer inserted into the centre comes out clean.

Allow to cool in the tin.

Rock Cakes

Makes about 24

250g self-raising flour
125g butter
125g sugar
½ cup sultanas
½ cup dates, chopped
½ cup chopped nuts
pinch of salt
½ teaspoon ground cinnamon
¼ teaspoon ground nutmeg
1 egg, lightly beaten
3 tablespoons milk

Heat the oven on to 160°C. Line 3 baking trays with baking paper.

In a large bowl, place the flour then add the butter and rub it into the flour with the fingertips until the mixture resembles breadcrumbs. Alternatively, use a food processor up to this stage and then transfer the mixture to a bowl. Add the sugar, sultanas, dates, nuts, salt, cinnamon and nutmeg and mix through.

In another bowl, whisk the egg and milk together. Mix into the flour mixture with a metal spoon until well combined.

Place heaped dessertspoonfuls of the mixture on the prepared trays, allowing a little room for spreading.

Bake for 12–15 minutes, or until the rock cakes are very lightly browned.

PASTA

(See also Minestrone, page 202.)

MACARONI CHEESE

Serves 4

4 cups milk
6 teaspoons cornflour mixed to a paste with ¼ cup of cold
   milk
125g grated tasty cheese
½ cup freshly grated parmesan cheese
1 dessertspoon chutney
1 dessertspoon tomato sauce (ketchup)
3 teaspoons vegetable stock powder
1 teaspoon Dijon mustard
3 cups cooked macaroni or similar
2 tablespoons chopped parsley

Pour the milk into a saucepan and bring to the boil. Thicken by whisking in some or all of the cornflour paste.

Add the cheeses, chutney, tomato sauce, stock powder and mustard, and mix well. Stir in the macaroni and barely simmer for 2 minutes until the pasta is heated through. Add the parsley and salt and pepper to taste.

CHEESY NOODLE BAKE

Serves 4

60g butter
125g bacon, diced
1 onion, diced
2 teaspoons curry powder
2 teaspoons chicken stock powder
2½ cups milk
2 teaspoons cornflour mixed to a paste with 1 tablespoon of
     cold milk
1 cup grated tasty cheese
1½–2 cups cooked pasta shells or spirals

Heat the oven to 180°C. Grease a 20cm casserole dish.

Melt the butter in a saucepan over medium heat and gently fry the bacon and onion until cooked.

Add the curry powder and stock powder and cook for 1 minute more.

Add the milk and bring to the boil. To thicken, add the cornflour paste while stirring continuously. Stir in the pasta and half of the grated cheese. Add salt and pepper to taste.

Pour into the prepared dish, top with the remaining grated cheese and bake for 20 minutes, or until golden.

VARIATIONS

- Extra vegetables can be added if desired. Just dice those of your choice and sauté with the onion and bacon.

- About 200g of cooked chicken or 125g of diced smoked salmon can also be added.

MACARONI BEEF AND TOMATO BAKE

Serves 6

1 tablespoon olive oil
300g best minced beef
1 large onion, diced
3 cloves garlic, crushed
1 red capsicum, diced
1 stick celery, diced
2 teaspoons curry powder
1 tablespoon chutney or relish
1 dessertspoon soy sauce
1 dessertspoon Worcestershire sauce
2 tablespoons tomato sauce (ketchup)
2 tablespoons tomato paste
400g tin crushed tomatoes
1 cup corn kernels
½ cup sliced olives (optional)
2 cups chicken, beef or vegetable stock
2 cups cooked pasta
¾ cup grated tasty cheese

Heat the oven to 170°C. Grease a 20cm casserole dish.

Heat the oil in a pot or frying pan over medium-high heat. Add the mince and cook, stirring, until the meat changes colour and is well broken up. Add the onion, garlic, capsicum and celery and cook gently for 3 minutes, then add the curry powder and cook a further 2 minutes.

Add the chutney, sauces, tomato paste, crushed tomatoes, corn, olives (if using) and stock. Bring back to the boil, stirring. Add the cooked pasta and mix in well. Season with salt and pepper to taste. Pour into the prepared casserole dish, sprinkle with the cheese and cover with foil.

Bake for 20 minutes, then remove the foil and bake for 10 minutes more, or until the cheese is melted and golden.

Napolitana Bake

Serves 4 as a side dish

2 tablespoons olive oil
1 large onion, finely diced
2 cloves garlic, crushed
1 teaspoon ground basil
1 teaspoon ground oregano
1 tablespoon white wine
1 teaspoon sugar
400g tin diced tomatoes
1 cup grated tasty cheese
2 cups cooked pasta
½ cup freshly grated or shaved parmesan cheese

Heat the oven to 170°C. Grease a 20cm casserole dish.

Heat the oil in a saucepan over medium heat and sauté the onion until soft, then add the garlic and cook for 1 minute more.

Add the herbs, wine, sugar, tomatoes, ½ cup of the grated cheese and salt and pepper to taste.

Heat until the cheese is melted.

Place the cooked pasta in the casserole dish, top with the sauce and mix well.

Sprinkle with the remaining ½ cup of tasty cheese and the parmesan cheese, then cover with foil.

Bake for 15 minutes, then remove foil and bake for 10 minutes more, or until the cheese on top is golden and bubbling.

CARBONARA

Serves 4

1 tablespoon olive oil
250g bacon, diced
3 cloves garlic, crushed
3 eggs
2 teaspoons cornflour
300ml cream
1 cup grated tasty cheese
½ cup freshly grated parmesan cheese
¼ teaspoon mustard powder or ½ teaspoon Dijon mustard
3 cups cooked spiralli or similar pasta
2 tablespoons chopped parsley

Heat the oil in a large saucepan over medium-high heat. Fry the bacon until crisp, then add the garlic and sauté for 1 minute more.

In a bowl whisk the eggs, cornflour and cream together until well combined, then add to the saucepan.

Cook over a very low heat, stirring constantly, until the sauce becomes thick. Mix in both cheeses and stir until melted. Stir in the mustard.

Stir in the pasta and cook over a low heat without boiling until the pasta is heated through.

Serve sprinkled with chopped parsley and/or extra parmesan cheese.

RICE

(See also: Koulibac with Lemon and Parsley Sauce, page 77;
Mushroom Risotto, page 165.)

Leftover cooked rice can spoil quite quickly so use it within 2 days. If it needs to be kept for longer, freeze it. It can remain frozen for up to 6 weeks.

Arancini Balls
(from leftover risotto)

Serves 4 (makes about 12 balls)

1 cup leftover risotto (chilled)
2 level teaspoons cornflour
1 egg yolk, lightly whisked
1 cup (approximately) fresh breadcrumbs
1 egg, lightly whisked
canola oil for deep frying

Mix the risotto, cornflour, egg yolk and 1½ tablespoons of the breadcrumbs. Roll into walnut-sized balls.

Roll the balls first in the egg, then in the remaining breadcrumbs. Place on a tray and refrigerate for 30 minutes.

Heat the oil in a saucepan or deep fryer to approximately 180°C and deep fry the arancini balls until crisp and golden. Drain on crumpled paper towel.

Serve with sweet chilli sauce and sour cream.

SAVOURY RICE PANCAKES

Makes 8–10

These savoury pancakes are very good served with crispy bacon. Try adding a little chopped chorizo or similar to the batter as well.

 ¼ teaspoon salt
 2 tablespoons chopped spring onion
 2 tablespoons chopped parsley
 2 tablespoons chopped semi-dried tomatoes
 ½ cup grated tasty cheese
 1 quantity rice pancake mixture (page 66)

Fold the salt, spring onion, parsley, tomato and cheese into the pancake mixture.

Heat a greased or non-stick frying pan over medium-high heat. Drop tablespoons of the mixture into the pan and cook for about 3 minutes, until golden on one side, then turn and cook on the other side for approximately 2 minutes, or until golden.

Serve with eggs, bacon, mushrooms and tomatoes.

FRIED RICE

Serves 2–4

1 tablespoon olive oil
150g lean bacon, diced
1 onion, finely diced
1 stick celery, finely diced
1 red capsicum, diced
3 eggs
2 cups cooked rice
1 tablespoon (approximately) soy sauce

Heat the oil in a wok or heavy-based frying pan over medium heat. Add the bacon and onion and sauté until the bacon begins to crisp and the onion is transparent. Add the celery and capsicum and cook for 1 minute more.

Turn heat to low and push the contents of the pan to one side. Break the eggs into the other side of pan and whisk lightly with a fork. Allow to cook on the base, then turn over to cook the other side. While still in the pan, cut into strips or small squares. Add the rice and mix all together. Cook over a low heat for 3–5 minutes, stirring gently once or twice, until the rice is heated through. Add the soy sauce to taste and stir to combine. Serve immediately.

PUMPKIN AND RICE CHOWDER

Serves 6

2 tablespoons olive oil
2 teaspoons butter
2 rashers bacon, diced
1 onion, diced
1 stick celery, diced
1 carrot, diced
750g pumpkin, peeled and cut into 1cm cubes
½ cooking apple (such as Granny Smith), peeled, cored and
    diced
5 cups chicken or vegetable stock
1 cup cooked rice
2 teaspoons cornflour mixed to a paste with 1½ tablespoons
    of cold water
½ cup grated tasty cheese
2 tablespoons shaved parmesan cheese
½ cup pouring cream

Heat the oil and butter in a large saucepan over medium-high heat and sauté the bacon until crispy. Add the onion, celery, carrot, pumpkin and apple and sauté over medium low heat for 5 minutes.

Pour in the stock and simmer until the vegetables are tender. Add the rice and bring back to the boil. Thicken by stirring in the cornflour paste. Mix in the cheeses and stir until melted. Remove from heat and stir in the cream. Add salt and white pepper to taste.

Top each serve of soup with chopped parsley.

RICE SALAD

Serves 2–4

2 teaspoons olive oil
2 rashers bacon, diced
2 cups cooked rice
2 spring onions, finely sliced
1 stick celery, finely diced
1 small red capsicum, finely diced
2 tablespoons chopped parsley
½ cup corn kernels (optional)
French dressing (see recipe below)
1 tablespoon mayonnaise

Heat the oil in a small saucepan over medium-high heat and sauté the bacon until crispy. Mix through the rice, together with the spring onion, celery, capsicum, parsley and corn, if using.

Mix in the French dressing, stand for 5 minutes then mix in the mayonnaise. Add salt and white pepper to taste.

French Dressing
1 tablespoon white vinegar
¼ teaspoon salt
pinch of mustard powder
¼ cup olive oil

Place all ingredients in a screw top jar and shake until well combined.

SPINACH, CHORIZO AND SEMI-DRIED TOMATO RICE BAKE

Serves 4

If preferred, this recipe can be made without the addition of the chorizo. It is then much more economical and is quite tasty enough without it.

2 teaspoons olive oil
90g chorizo, finely diced
2 eggs
½ teaspoon salt
pinch of nutmeg
1 onion, very finely chopped or grated
½ cup grated tasty cheese
1 teaspoon Worcestershire sauce
1 teaspoon chopped fresh thyme or ½ teaspoon dried
1 cup finely shredded silver beet or spinach
½ cup chopped semi-dried tomatoes
½ cup milk
2 cups cooked rice (brown or white)

Topping
125g chopped bacon
1 tablespoon melted butter
½ cup grated parmesan cheese (optional)

Heat the oven to 170°C. Grease an 18cm casserole dish.

Heat the oil in a frying pan over medium-high heat and cook the chorizo until it begins to crisp. Remove the chorizo.

Whisk the eggs in a large bowl, add the salt, nutmeg, onion, cheese, Worcestershire sauce, thyme, silver beet, tomatoes, milk, rice and chorizo, and mix together very well.

Pour into the prepared casserole dish and top with the chopped bacon, then drizzle over the melted butter and top with parmesan, if using.

Bake for approximately 40 minutes, or until set.

Serve with a green or Greek salad.

SPANISH RICE

Serves 4

2 tablespoons olive oil
1 onion, finely diced
2 red capsicums, diced
1 chorizo, finely chopped
1 stick celery, sliced
2 spring onions, finely sliced
1 cup corn kernels
3 cups cooked rice
2 tablespoons chopped parsley

Heat the oil in a frying pan over medium-high heat and sauté the onion, capsicum, chorizo and celery until the onion is transparent and the chorizo begins to crisp. Add the spring onion and corn and cook for 1 minute more.

Stir in the rice and parsley, heat through and serve.

STUFFED CAPSICUMS

Serves 4

4 red capsicums
600g best minced beef
1 egg, lightly whisked
1 onion, grated
1 tablespoon chopped parsley
1 large clove garlic, crushed
1 cup cooked rice
2 rashers bacon, finely diced
2 tablespoons tomato paste
2 teaspoons sweet chilli sauce
2 teaspoons Worcestershire sauce
1 teaspoon salt
410g tin diced tomatoes
½ teaspoon brown sugar
1 cup grated tasty cheese

Heat the oven to 180°C. Grease an 18cm x 28cm lasagne dish.

Cut the capsicums in half lengthways and remove the seeds.

Mix together the mince, egg, onion, parsley, garlic, rice, bacon,
1 tablespoon of the tomato paste, sweet chilli sauce, Worcestershire sauce
and ¾ teaspoon of the salt. Fill the capsicum halves with this mixture.
Place the capsicums in the prepared dish.

Mix together the remaining tomato paste and salt with the tomatoes and
sugar and spoon over the capsicums. Sprinkle with the cheese and bake
for 30 minutes until the meat is cooked through and the cheese is lightly
browned.

Serve with a green or Greek salad.

TOMATO RICE FLAN

Serves 4–6

1 tablespoon olive oil
2 rashers bacon, finely diced
1 small onion, finely diced
2 eggs
½ cup cream or milk
½ cup plain or Greek yoghurt (or extra milk)
¾ teaspoon salt
2 teaspoons mayonnaise
3 teaspoons cornflour
2 tomatoes, diced
2 spring onions, finely sliced
1 cup grated tasty cheese
2 tablespoons grated parmesan cheese
2 cups cooked rice
2 tablespoons finely chopped parsley

Heat the oven to 150°C. Grease a 23cm pie dish.

Heat the oil in a small saucepan over medium-high heat. Sauté the onion and bacon until the onion is transparent and the bacon begins to crisp.

Whisk together the eggs, cream, yoghurt, salt, mayonnaise and cornflour.

In a large bowl, mix together the bacon mixture, egg mixture, tomatoes, spring onions, cheeses, rice and parsley. Combine well and pour into the prepared dish.

Bake for 30–40 minutes, or until set. Allow to stand for 10 minutes before cutting into wedges to serve.

Serve with a green or Greek salad, or with seasonal vegetables.

BAKED FRUITY RICE CUSTARD

Serves 4–6

1½ cups cooked rice
1 teaspoon finely grated lemon rind
¼ cup currants
¼ cup raisins
¼ cup chopped dried apricots
½ cup sugar
3 eggs
2 cups milk
½ teaspoon vanilla extract or essence
½ teaspoon ground nutmeg
1 teaspoon butter, diced

Heat the oven to 140°C. Grease a 20cm casserole dish and have ready a baking dish in which the casserole dish will comfortably fit.

Mix together the rice, lemon rind, currants, raisins and dried apricots and spoon into the prepared casserole dish.

In a bowl whisk together the sugar and eggs until well combined, then whisk in the milk and vanilla. Pour over the rice and fruit mixture. Sprinkle nutmeg over the top and dot with the small pieces of butter.

Place the casserole dish in the baking dish and pour warm water around the casserole dish to a depth of 3cm.

Bake for 1½ hours, or until the custard is set.

Serve with vanilla ice cream. If any of the pudding is left over, refrigerate overnight and serve with fresh fruit for breakfast next morning.

RICE PANCAKES WITH BLUEBERRY SAUCE

Makes about 8

These pancakes are delicious for breakfast – more substantial than a regular hotcake with the handy inclusion of leftover cooked rice. A savoury version on page 57 is also delicious.

Pancake Mix
1 cup milk
1 egg
1 cup self-raising flour
1 cup cooked rice

Blueberry* Sauce
1½–2 cups blueberries, fresh or frozen
¼ cup sugar
¼ cup water
1½ teaspoons cornflour mixed to a paste with 2 tablespoons
    of cold water

In a bowl whisk the milk and egg together, then whisk in the flour until smooth. Fold in the rice.

Heat a greased or non-stick frying pan over medium-high heat. Drop tablespoons of the mixture into the pan and cook for about 3 minutes, until golden on one side, then turn and cook on the other side for approximately 2 minutes, or until golden.

To make the sauce, place the blueberries and sugar in a small saucepan with the water, bring to the boil and simmer over a gentle heat for 5 minutes. Add the cornflour paste and stir until thickened slightly. Add extra sugar if needed.

Serve sauce drizzled over the pancakes.

* *You can substitute any type of berry for the blueberries.*

QUEEN OF RICE PUDDINGS

Serves 4–6

3 eggs
½ cup sugar
2 cups milk
½ teaspoon vanilla extract or essence
1–1¼ cups cooked rice
½ cup raspberry jam
3 egg whites
⅔ cup sugar

Heat oven to 150°C. Grease a 20cm casserole dish and have ready a baking dish in which the casserole dish will comfortably fit.

In a bowl whisk the eggs and sugar together until well combined, then whisk in the milk and vanilla.

Place the rice in the prepared dish and pour the egg mixture over.

Place the casserole dish in the baking dish and pour warm water around the casserole dish to a depth of 3cm.

Place in the oven and bake for 1 hour, or until the custard is set. Remove from the oven and leave to stand for 5 minutes. Spread with the raspberry jam.

Beat the egg whites until soft peaks form, then add the sugar and beat until stiff peaks form. Spoon over the pudding and swirl decoratively with a knife. Reduce the oven temperature to 140°C and bake for 20 minutes more, or until the topping is lightly browned.

Serve with vanilla ice cream or mascarpone.

FISH, POULTRY & MEAT

Whenever there are leftovers of these foods, it is important to cover and refrigerate them as soon as possible, and then to use them within 3 days, or frozen and used within 4 weeks.

When a leftover is reheated as part of another dish, it is important to make sure it is thoroughly heated through. So if it is to be boiled, bring it to the boil and simmer for a minimum of two minutes.

Many casseroles, stews and especially curries taste better the next day when the flavours are fully developed. They make excellent pie fillings.

Leftover gravy can be stored in small containers in the fridge or freezer. Add gravy leftover to casserole-type dishes for an extra flavour boost, but add it at the start of cooking. The same applies to small amounts of leftover soups.

In all the chicken recipes in this section, turkey or duck can be substituted.

Leftover pieces of smallgoods can be stored in the fridge for 4 days, or in the freezer for up to 4 weeks, to use later as pizza toppings or in casseroles.

Lately I have discovered an absolutely delicious way to use leftover sausages: wrap them in bread dough. To make the dough, mix together well 2 cups of plain flour, 2 teaspoons of dried yeast, 1½ teaspoons of sugar, 1 teaspoon of salt, 2 teaspoons of oil and 1 cup of warm water. Allow it to rise in the bowl (covered with a tea towel) for 50 minutes, then turn it out onto a lightly floured surface and knead briefly, cut the dough into 6 pieces and wrap each piece around the 6 cooked sausages. Leave to rise on 2 greased 2 x 30cm baking trays for 20 minutes, then bake at 200°C for 12–15 minutes, or until the dough is cooked. They can be eaten immediately, split in half with sauce or chutney added, or allowed to cool and filled with salad.

Use the bone from a leg of ham to make a delicious pea and ham soup, or add to beef, chicken or pork casseroles for a different flavour.

Save the bones from a roast of lamb, pork, beef or poultry to make soup. Specific instructions are given in the recipes of this section. Beef, lamb and pork bones are interchangeable, and turkey or duck bones can be substituted for chicken bones.

Fish bones can also be used to make stock – this should not be cooked for any longer than 20 minutes. The exception to this is shellfish (such as lobster shells) which should be cooked for about 2 hours to extract maximum flavour.

FISH

(See also Crispy Fish Tart, page 30.)

Place cooked fish in the fridge as soon as it has cooled after cooking.

There is no need to discard fish bones; they can be used to make a tasty stock for use later. If a clear stock is needed, it is best to use the bones of non-oily white fish.

To make fish stock, simply rinse any traces of blood from the bones, then chop roughly and place in a saucepan and cover with cold water. Bring to the boil, then reduce heat and simmer for 20 minutes only, removing any scum that rises to the top. Strain. If you want to flavour the stock, add some onion, carrot, celery and parsley stalks at the outset.

To make stock from lobster shells or similar, use the same method but cook for 2 hours at least.

Store in airtight containers in the fridge for up to 3 days, or freeze for up to 2 months.

EASY FISH CURRY

Serves 4

30g butter
2–3 teaspoons curry powder
2 teaspoons chicken or vegetable stock powder
3 cups milk
2 teaspoons smooth-textured chutney
6 teaspoons cornflour mixed to a paste with 3 tablespoons of
　　milk
¾ cup grated tasty cheese
300–400g cooked fish, cut into cubes

Melt the butter in a saucepan and add the curry and stock powders. Cook gently for 1 minute.

Add the milk and bring to the boil. Thicken by stirring in the cornflour paste, then mix in the chutney and grated cheese.

Add the fish and simmer for barely 2 minutes, or until heated through.

Serve with plain boiled rice, lemon wedges and salad.

FISH PATTIES

Serves 4

300g (approximately) flaked cooked fish
1 onion, grated
½ cup self-raising flour
½ cup milk
2 eggs, lightly whisked
¼ teaspoon salt
2 teaspoons lemon juice
2 teaspoons chopped dill or parsley (optional)
3 tablespoons canola or peanut oil for frying

Mix together all the ingredients in a bowl, except for the oil.

Heat the oil in a frying pan over medium-high heat. Place tablespoons of the batter in the frying pan, allowing a little room between the patties for spreading. Cook for 3 minutes on one side, then turn and cook for about 2 minutes on the other side, or until golden brown. Drain on absorbent paper.

Serve with tomato sauce, chutney or mayonnaise.

FISH PASTIES

Makes 12

These pasties are delicious served with tomato chutney.

350g (approximately) cooked fish, flaked or diced
1 chorizo, finely diced
250g cooked diced vegetables (or just potato)
1 spring onion, finely diced (optional)
1 onion, grated
2 teaspoons lemon juice
½ teaspoon Dijon mustard
2 teaspoons whole-egg mayonnaise
1 tomato, deseeded and diced
1 tablespoon chopped parsley
3 sheets frozen puff or shortcrust pastry, thawed*
60g butter, cut into 12 small cubes

Heat the oven to 200°C. Line 2 baking trays with baking paper.

In a large bowl, mix together the fish, chorizo, vegetables, spring onion, onion, lemon juice, mustard, mayonnaise, tomato and parsley.

Cut each pastry sheet into 4 squares and place a spoonful of filling on each. Top with a piece of butter. Dampen 2 edges of each parcel and fold over diagonally to make 4 triangles. Seal the edges and place on the prepared trays. Prick each pasty once with a fork.

Bake for 20 minutes, or until puffed and golden.

* *Or make your own shortcrust pastry from the recipe on page 233.*

CREAMY SEAFOOD MORNAY

Serves 4

90g butter
1 onion, finely diced
4 tablespoons plain flour
3 cups milk
1 cup grated tasty cheese
500g cooked seafood, cubed if fillets
1 cup cooked or tinned corn kernels (optional)
1 cup cooked fresh or frozen peas (optional)

In a frying pan, melt the butter over medium heat and sauté the onion until soft. Add the flour and cook for 1 minute longer, stirring.

Gradually whisk in the milk, stirring constantly. Bring to the boil and simmer for 3 minutes, or until thickened, whisking constantly.

Add the cheese, seafood, and corn and peas, if using, and salt and pepper to taste. Simmer gently for 2 minutes.

Serve with seasonal vegetables, or plain boiled rice and green salad.

VARIATIONS

• Top with crushed cornflakes, dot with small pieces of butter and bake for 20 minutes at 180°C.

• Alternatively, fill thin pancakes (see recipe on the next page) with the seafood mixture, roll up, place side by side in a baking dish, sprinkle with ½–1 cup of extra grated tasty cheese and bake for 15 minutes at 160°C, or until the cheese is melted.

Pancakes
Makes 6—8
125g plain flour
½ teaspoon salt
1 egg
250–300ml water or milk

In a large bowl, mix the flour and salt together. Make a well in the centre and all at once add the egg and enough water or milk to make a thin batter.

Whisk until smooth, then leave to stand for 30 minutes if possible.

Lightly grease a small frying pan, or lightly spray with cooking oil, and heat over medium heat. Pour in about 2 tablespoons of the pancake batter and spread over the base of the pan.

Cook on one side until lightly golden, then turn with a spatula or egg flip to briefly cook the other (do not allow the pancakes to brown).

KEDGEREE

Serves 4

Kedgeree is known and served as a traditional English-style breakfast dish. However, it can be served any time of the day and makes excellent use of leftover fish. I also find the addition of some chopped semi-dried tomatoes a tasty option.

90g butter
1 onion, finely diced
2–3 cups leftover cooked flaked fish
3 hard boiled eggs, chopped
3 cups cooked rice
3 teaspoons lemon juice
½ cup finely chopped parsley

In a frying pan, melt the butter over low-medium heat and gently sauté the onion until transparent.

Mix in the fish, eggs, rice, lemon juice and parsley. Add salt and white pepper to taste. Cook gently for 3–5 minutes, turning the mixture frequently with a fork or spatula, until thoroughly heated through.

KOULIBAC WITH LEMON AND PARSLEY SAUCE

Serves 4

1 cup baby spinach leaves or shredded spinach or silver beet
500g well-flavoured cooked fish, such as salmon, flaked
1 egg, lightly whisked
1 tablespoon lemon juice
½ cup grated tasty cheese
2 teaspoons whole-egg mayonnaise
2 tablespoons cream or sour cream
2 tablespoons chopped parsley
1 onion, grated
2 cups cooked rice
4 hard boiled eggs
2 sheets frozen puff pastry, thawed

Lemon and Parsley Sauce
300ml milk
3 teaspoons cornflour mixed to a paste with 2 tablespoons of
    cold milk
2 teaspoons butter, diced
½ teaspoon salt
1 tablespoon chopped parsley
1 tablespoon lemon juice
1 tablespoon shaved parmesan cheese (or grated tasty
    cheese)

Heat the oven to 200°C. Grease a 30cm x 30cm baking tray.

Pour boiling water over the spinach or silver beet and leave to stand for
3 minutes. Drain well and squeeze out excess liquid.

In a bowl mix together the fish, whisked egg, lemon juice, cheese, mayonnaise, cream, parsley, onion and rice. Dice the hard boiled eggs into 1cm cubes and carefully fold into the fish mixture.

Place 1 sheet of the pastry on the prepared baking tray. Spoon the filling onto this, leaving a 1cm pastry strip around the edges. Dampen the edges with water or a little egg white. Place the remaining sheet of pastry over the top and press the edges together (you may need to stretch the top layer of pastry just a little to make it fit).

Bake for 30 minutes, or until the pastry is puffed and golden.

To make the lemon and parsley sauce, heat the milk in a saucepan to boiling, then whisk in the cornflour paste to thicken. Whisk in the butter, then add the salt, parsley, lemon juice and parmesan or tasty cheese.

Serve Koulibac with the sauce to the side with a green salad.

SEAFOOD CHOWDER

Serves 4

350g cooked fish
3 cups milk
5 teaspoons cornflour mixed to a paste with ½ cup of cold milk
2 teaspoons whole-egg mayonnaise
½ cup grated tasty cheese
1 tablespoon lemon juice
½ cup pouring cream
snipped chives to serve

Cut the fish into bite-sized pieces.

Place the milk in a saucepan and bring to the boil, then whisk in the cornflour paste, stirring until it thickens. Mix through the mayonnaise and cheese until melted. Add the prepared fish and heat through. Stir in the lemon juice and cream, and keep hot but do not boil. Add salt and white pepper to taste.

Serve each portion with a sprinkling of snipped chives.

CHICKEN AND OTHER POULTRY

It is really important to make sure that chicken is covered and refrigerated as soon as possible after cooking. Leftover chicken has a tendency to dry out, so the following recipes have been designed to rehydrate the chicken with tasty sauces.

After cooking a roast chicken, I take any leftover meat off the bones before covering and refrigerating, and use the bones to make a plain chicken stock for later use. To do this, simply cover the bones with water, bring to the boil and simmer for 2 hours*. Strain out the bones and discard, then cool the stock as quickly as possible and refrigerate. The fat can be easily lifted off the surface the next day. Use the stock within 3 days or place in smaller containers and freeze for up to 2 months.

For an additional recipe, see Chicken and Vegetable Strudel (page 236) which can be easily adapted for leftover chicken.

In the following recipes, other poultry such as turkey and duck can be substituted for chicken.

*Hint: *Alternatively, place the bones in a slow cooker with 2 cups of water and cook on high for 3 hours.*

Chicken à la King

Serves 4

2 tablespoons olive oil
250g mushrooms, sliced
1 red capsicum, diced
1 cup chicken stock
1 teaspoon sweet paprika
2 teaspoons lemon juice
2 teaspoons sherry
½ teaspoon salt
2 egg yolks
1 teaspoon Dijon mustard
3 teaspoons cornflour
200ml milk or cream
250–300g (approximately) cooked chicken, diced

Heat the oil in a saucepan over medium-high heat and sauté the mushrooms and capsicum for 5 minutes. Add the chicken stock and bring to the boil. Simmer for 5 minutes.

Meanwhile, in a bowl whisk together the paprika, lemon juice, sherry, salt, egg yolks, mustard, cornflour and milk or cream. Add to the mushroom mixture and stir until thickened. Stir in the chicken, bring to the boil and simmer gently for 3 minutes more.

Serve with buttered noodles and/or fresh seasonal vegetables.

CHICKEN AND ALMONDS

Serves 4

1 tablespoon olive oil
2 cups sliced mushrooms
1 small onion, diced
2 cloves garlic, crushed
2 teaspoons tomato paste
2 teaspoons tomato sauce (ketchup)
1 cup chicken stock
2 teaspoons cornflour mixed to a thin paste with 1 tablespoon
   of cold water
300g (approximately) cooked chicken, diced
½–1 cup slivered almonds
¼ cup pouring or thickened cream

In a saucepan heat the oil over medium-high heat and sauté the mushrooms and onion for 5 minutes. Add the garlic and sauté for 1 minute more.

Add the tomato paste, tomato sauce and stock. Simmer for 10 minutes. Thicken by stirring in all or some of the cornflour paste.

Mix in the chicken and almonds and simmer gently for 3 minutes. Stir in the cream and salt and white pepper to taste.

Serve with plain boiled or steamed rice and seasonal vegetables.

Chicken and Mushroom Pie

Serves 4

1 tablespoon oil
2 cups sliced mushrooms
1 onion, diced
2 cloves garlic
2 teaspoons tomato paste
2 teaspoons sweet paprika
1 teaspoon Dijon mustard
1 cup chicken stock
300g cooked chicken, diced
3 teaspoons cornflour mixed to a paste with 1 tablespoon of
 cold water
½ cup sour cream
1 sheet frozen puff pastry, thawed

Heat the oven to 200°C. Grease a 20cm casserole or pie dish.

In a saucepan heat the oil over medium-high heat and sauté the
mushrooms and onion for 5 minutes. Add the garlic and sauté for 1 minute
more. Mix in the tomato paste, paprika, mustard and stock. Simmer for
10 minutes.

Add the chicken, bring to the boil and thicken by stirring in all or some of
the cornflour paste. Stir in the sour cream. Add salt and pepper to taste.
Remove from heat and pour into the prepared casserole dish.

Place the pastry sheet over the top of the chicken and mushroom mixture.
Bake for 20–25 minutes, or until the pastry is puffed and golden.

TILLY'S CHICKEN CURRY

Serves 4

This recipe came about as an adaptation of Tilly's Indian Beef curry, a recipe from *Slow Cooker*. Tilly's son David created this most pleasing version of his mother's recipe. The moist sauce gives new life to yesterday's chicken, which can sometimes be a little dry.

    1 onion
    2 carrots
    1 stick celery
    2 apples
    2 tablespoons olive oil
    1 tablespoon sultanas
    1 tablespoon chutney
    1 tablespoon tomato sauce (ketchup)
    1 tablespoon Worcestershire sauce
    1 tablespoon golden syrup
    2 tablespoons brown sugar
    1 tablespoon curry powder or curry paste
    1½ cups water or chicken stock
    300g (approximately) cooked chicken, diced
    2 teaspoons cornflour, mixed to a paste with 2 tablespoons of
        cold water

Peel the onion and carrots and cut into 1cm cubes. Cut the celery into 1cm slices. Peel, core and dice the apples. In a saucepan heat the oil over medium heat and sauté the vegetables and apple for 5 minutes, stirring often.

Add the sultanas, chutney, sauces, golden syrup, brown sugar, curry powder and water or chicken stock. Bring to the boil and simmer for 5 minutes, then add the chicken, bring back to the boil and simmer for 5 minutes more. If it needs to be thickened, stir in some or all of the cornflour paste, stirring until it thickens. Add salt and pepper to taste.

Serve with plain boiled rice.

SPANISH CHICKEN

Serves 4

1 tablespoon olive oil
1 onion, peeled and diced
1 capsicum, diced
2 cloves garlic, crushed
1 teaspoon allspice powder
1 tablespoon lemon juice
2 teaspoon Dijon or wholegrain mustard
2 teaspoons Worcestershire sauce
425g good quality tomato soup
425g can corn kernels, drained
½ cup sliced Kalamata olives
250–350g cooked chicken, diced

In a saucepan heat the oil over medium-high heat and sauté the onion and capsicum until softened. Add the garlic and sauté for 1 minute more.

Add the rest of the ingredients except for the chicken. Bring to the boil and simmer for 3 minutes, then add the chicken, bring to the boil again and simmer for 3 minutes more. Add salt and pepper to taste.

Serve with steamed rice and green salad.

TOMATO CURRY CHICKEN

Serves 4

1 tablespoon oil
125g bacon, diced
1 capsicum, diced
1 onion, diced
3 teaspoons curry powder or curry paste
2 cups tinned diced tomatoes
1 cup chicken stock or water
2 tablespoons tomato paste
1 dessertspoon soy sauce
1 dessertspoon Worcestershire sauce
1 tablespoon sweet chilli sauce
2 teaspoons chutney
300g (approximately) cooked chicken, diced

Heat the oil in a wok over medium-high heat and sauté the bacon, capsicum and onion for 5 minutes while stirring. Mix in the curry powder and sauté for 1 minute more.

Add the rest of the ingredients except for the chicken, bring to the boil, then simmer until the sauce is reduced by one third. Add the chicken, bring to the boil and simmer for 4 minutes, or until the chicken is heated through. Add salt and pepper to taste.

Serve with plain boiled rice and salad.

Chicken Biryani

Serves 4

2 tablespoons olive oil
2 onions, finely diced
1 tablespoon crushed garlic
1 tablespoon finely grated fresh ginger
2 teaspoons ground cumin
1 teaspoon ground coriander
½ teaspoon ground cinnamon
¼ teaspoon ground cardamom
1 teaspoon salt
1 tablespoon sweet chilli sauce
400g diced tomatoes, fresh, tinned, frozen or bottled
1 tablespoon tomato paste
250–300g diced cooked chicken
3 cups cooked rice

In a saucepan heat the oil over medium heat and sauté the onion until translucent, add the garlic and ginger and sauté for 1 minute more. Add the spices and sauté for 1 minute, then add the salt, sweet chilli sauce, tomatoes and tomato paste. Bring to the boil and simmer for 5 minutes, then stir in the chicken.

Heat the oven to 160°C. Grease an 18–20cm round casserole dish.

Place one third of the rice in the base, then one third of the sauce. Repeat the layering process twice. Cover with foil and bake for 30 minutes.

Serve with green salad or seasonal vegetables.

Chicken and Pine Nut Risotto

Serves 2–4

1 tablespoon olive oil
2 teaspoons butter
1 onion, finely diced
1 cup arborio rice
750ml hot chicken or vegetable stock
½ cup corn kernels or creamed corn
½–¾ cup pine nuts
250–300g cooked chicken, diced
¼ cup cream
60g butter, extra
½ cup freshly grated parmesan cheese

In a saucepan heat the oil and the 2 teaspoons of butter over medium heat and sauté the onion until transparent. Add the rice and stir to coat.

Add 1 cup of the stock to the rice and cook until the liquid is absorbed, stirring often. Continue adding the stock 1 cup at a time until all of it is used and the rice is tender. Stir in the corn, pine nuts and chicken and cook for 3 minutes more.

Stir through the cream, extra butter and parmesan, and salt and white pepper to taste.

MEAT

After you have cooked roast lamb, beef or pork with the bone in, don't just throw the bone away. Instead, make your own stock, which can be done very simply and saves the expense of the commercial variety. I place mine in the slow cooker with 3 cups of water, an onion, carrot, celery, a bay leaf and I teaspoon of salt and cook it on High for 4 hours or 8–9 hours on Low. Alternatively, you can add 4 cups water and cook the stock on the stovetop. Strain and cool. Place in a covered container in the fridge. When cold, simply lift off the fat and your stock is ready to be used. It will keep in the fridge for 4 days and can be frozen for up to 2 months.

Use leftover casseroles and curries as individual pie fillings. I remember being introduced as a child to the wonder of a 'jaffle iron'. I guess this was the olden day equivalent of a pie maker. Thin slices of buttered bread were placed in each side of the jaffle iron, with the butter side against the iron, and leftover stew was spooned in and then the iron was closed. It was then put in the coals of the open fire until the bread was golden brown to make a 'pie'. I clearly remember thinking that it was the most delicious thing I had ever tasted. Probably this was because stews and casseroles often have a better flavour next day, but more likely it was the cooking over the hot coals. It was as good as any pie of today; nothing yet has come up to the standard of the ones made with bread in that old jaffle iron.

There are also recipes on pages 102 through to 106 for using up leftover sausages and other barbecued meats.

Beef – roasted

♦

BEEF IN TOMATO SAUCE

Serves 4

2 tablespoons olive oil
1 large onion, finely diced
1 clove garlic, crushed
400g tin diced tomatoes
1 tablespoon tomato sauce (ketchup)
2 teaspoons Worcestershire sauce
3 teaspoons sweet chilli sauce
2 teaspoons chopped fresh rosemary or thyme (optional)
¾ cup beef or chicken stock
2 teaspoons cornflour mixed to a paste with 2 tablespoons of
     cold water
**300g (approximately) cooked roast or pot roast beef, cut
     into 1cm cubes**

In a large saucepan, heat the oil over medium heat and sauté the onion
until soft. Add the garlic and sauté for 1 minute more. Add the tomatoes,
sauces, herbs and stock and bring to the boil. Simmer for 5 minutes.

Thicken by whisking in some or all of the cornflour paste, stirring until it
thickens. Add the beef and simmer gently for 3 minutes or until heated
through. Add salt and pepper to taste.

Hint: *Leftover meatballs or patties can be substituted for cooked roast beef.*

Fragrant Spiced Beef

Serves 4

1 tablespoon olive oil
1 onion, diced
2 cloves garlic, crushed
1 tablespoon ground cumin
2 teaspoons ground coriander
2 teaspoons ground turmeric
¼ teaspoon ground cloves
1 piece star anise
425g tin diced tomatoes
½ cup beef, chicken or vegetable stock or water
500g (approximately) cooked roast beef
3 teaspoons cornflour mixed to a paste with 2 tablespoons of
    cold water

Heat the oil in a large saucepan over medium heat and sauté the onion until soft. Add the garlic and sauté for 1 minute more. Add the cumin, coriander, turmeric and cloves and cook for 1 minute, stirring. Add the star anise, tomatoes and stock or water. Bring to the boil and simmer for 10 minutes.

Meanwhile, cut the beef into 1cm cubes. Add to the simmering sauce, bring back to the boil and simmer for 5 minutes more. Add salt and pepper to taste. If it needs to be thickened, stir in some or all of the cornflour paste, stirring until it thickens. Remove the star anise.

Serve with plain steamed rice and salad or seasonal vegetables.

Beef – minced dishes

If you have a leftover mince dish, such as curried mince, chilli con carne or savoury mince, there are many ways it can be used. For instance, it can be used as a filling for individual pies made in a pie maker or oven. Alternatively, if you have about 2 cupfuls, pour this into a greased 18cm–20cm casserole or pie dish and cover with mashed potatoes topped with a handful of grated tasty cheese. Of course, a whole sheet of thawed frozen puff pastry can be used instead of the mashed potato. In either case, bake for 20 minutes at 200°C. Any Mexican-style spicy mince can be used as a filling for tacos or a topping for nachos.

◆

EMPANADAS

Serves 4

1 sheet frozen puff pastry, thawed
1 cup (approximately) leftover cooked mince
1 tablespoon sour cream
2 tablespoons grated tasty cheese

Heat the oven to 200°C. Grease a 30cm x 30cm baking tray.

Cut the pastry into 4 squares. Spoon the mince into the centre of each square and top each with a teaspoon of sour cream and sprinkle with the grated cheese.

Dampen two edges of each and fold over diagonally to make 4 triangles.

Bake for 15–20 minutes, or until the pastry is puffed and golden.

Serve with sweet chilli sauce and vegetables.

Beef – corned

Both these versions were very popular with our children when they were young.

—————————— ◆ ——————————

BURDEKIN DUCK I

Serves 4

2 eggs, lightly whisked
1½ cups self-raising flour
1¼ cups milk
¼ teaspoon salt
¼ teaspoon mustard powder (optional)
250g (approximately) finely diced cooked corned beef
1 tablespoon snipped chives or 1 teaspoon grated onion
   (optional)
½ cup (approximately) canola or peanut oil for frying

In a bowl whisk together the eggs, flour, milk, salt and mustard until the mixture is smooth. Stir in the corned beef and chives or onion, if using.

Heat the oil in a large frying pan over medium-high heat. Drop rounded tablespoonfuls of the mixture into the hot oil and cook for 3 minutes, or until golden on one side and bubbles begin to appear on the surface. Turn with a spatula or egg flip and cook for 2 minutes on the other side, until golden.

Serve with tomato sauce or chutney and fresh seasonal vegetables or salad.

BURDEKIN DUCK 2

Serves 4

250g (approximately) cooked corned silverside
¾ cup self-raising flour
¼ teaspoon salt
pinch of bicarbonate of soda
½ cup canola or peanut oil for frying

Cut the corned beef into 3mm slices.

In a bowl whisk together the flour, salt, bicarbonate of soda and enough cold water to make a good coating consistency. Leave to stand for 30 minutes if possible.

Heat the oil in a frying pan over medium-high heat. Dip the slices of corned beef in the batter and cook in the oil on one side for 2 minutes, or until golden, then turn and cook the other side until golden. Drain on absorbent kitchen paper.

Serve with seasonal vegetables or a green salad and tomato sauce or chutney.

CORNED BEEF HASH

Serves 4

600g potatoes, peeled and cut into 2cm cubes
30g butter
½ teaspoon (approximately) salt
2 tablespoons oil
1 onion, peeled and finely diced
1½ cups diced cooked corned beef
½ teaspoon Dijon, English or American mustard
2 eggs, lightly whisked
1 tablespoon self-raising flour
2 tablespoons finely chopped parsley

Cook the potatoes in boiling salted water until just tender. Drain and mash with the butter and salt. The mixture does not need to be extremely smooth.

Heat the oil in a frying pan over medium heat and sauté the onion until soft. Mix the potato, corned beef, mustard, eggs and flour in a bowl and then add to the onion. Cook over medium-high heat until browned underneath, then turn over and cook until the other side is brown.

Serve sprinkled with the chopped parsley.

Lamb

(See also Spicy Lamb Triangles, page 101.)

♦

SHEPHERD'S PIE

Serves 4–6

500g cooked roast lamb
1 onion
1 tablespoon plain flour
¼ cup tomato sauce (ketchup)
½ teaspoon dried thyme
1 cup milk
2 tablespoons leftover gravy (if available)
750g potatoes, peeled, cut in to 5cm cubes
60g butter
½ cup milk, extra
1 egg
½ teaspoon (approximately) salt
½ cup grated tasty cheese

Heat the oven to 170°C. Grease a 20cm casserole or deep pie dish.

Mince or process in a food processor or chop very finely the lamb and the onion together. Add the flour, tomato sauce, thyme, milk, gravy and salt and pepper to taste. Mix well. Spoon evenly into the prepared dish.

Meanwhile, cook the potato in a little boiling water until very soft. Drain and mash well. Quickly whisk in the butter, extra milk, egg and salt, mixing until very smooth. Spread over the meat and sprinkle with grated cheese. Bake for 30 minutes, or until heated through and the cheese is golden.

Serve with a little extra tomato sauce and fresh seasonal vegetables.

TANDOORI LAMB

Serves 4

1 tablespoon olive oil
2 onions, finely diced
3 cloves garlic, crushed
1 teaspoon grated green ginger root
2 teaspoons garam masala
1 teaspoon paprika
1 teaspoon ground cardamom
1 teaspoon ground coriander
1 teaspoon ground cumin
1 tablespoon chutney (any sort)
3 teaspoons sweet chilli sauce
½ teaspoon salt
2 teaspoons tomato paste or 1 tablespoon tomato sauce
   (ketchup)
2 cups chicken stock or water
300g cubed cooked lamb
2 teaspoons cornflour mixed to a paste with 1 tablespoon of
   cold water
2 tablespoons Greek or plain yoghurt

Heat the oil in a saucepan over medium heat and sauté the onion until soft. Add the garlic and ginger and sauté for 1 minute more. Stir in the spices and gently cook for 1 minute, then add the chutney, chilli sauce, salt, tomato paste and stock. Bring to the boil and simmer for 10 minutes.

Add the lamb and simmer gently for 5 minutes. Thicken by mixing in some or all of the cornflour paste, stirring until it thickens, and then stir in the yoghurt. Add salt and pepper to taste.

Serve over steamed or boiled rice.

Pork

♦

CRISPY PORK WITH GARLIC AND GINGER SAUCE AND RED CABBAGE BRAISE

Serves 6

When cooking this dish it is important to have the oil hot enough to cook and crisp the batter and reheat the pork without over-cooking it. The red cabbage braise is the perfect accompaniment. Parsnip mash matches well also, the recipe for which follows.

    1 cup self-raising flour
    ⅛ teaspoon bicarbonate of soda
    ¼ teaspoon salt
    1 tablespoon light olive oil
    2 tablespoons grated green ginger root
    3 cloves garlic, crushed
    ¼ cup sugar
    ¼ cup cider vinegar
    ½ cup water
    1 tablespoon soy sauce
    2 teaspoons sherry
    ½ teaspoon salt, extra
    2 teaspoons cornflour
    1 cup canola oil for deep frying
    300g leftover roast pork, cut into 1cm cubes

To make the batter, sift the flour, bicarbonate of soda and salt into a bowl and mix in enough cold water to make a good coating consistency. Leave to stand for 30 minutes if possible.

Meanwhile, heat the olive oil in a frying pan over medium heat and sauté the ginger and garlic for 2 minutes. Add the sugar, vinegar, water, soy sauce, sherry, extra salt and cornflour and bring to the boil. Simmer for 2 minutes. Remove from heat and keep warm.

Heat the canola oil in a saucepan to approximately 180°C. Dip the pork cubes into the batter then deep fry in the oil, a few at a time, for about 2 minutes, or until crispy. Drain on absorbent kitchen paper.

Serve the pork, drizzled with the sauce.

Red Cabbage Braise
Serves 6

2 medium leeks, white part only
1 tablespoon olive oil
1 teaspoon butter
150g diced bacon
1 onion, peeled and finely diced
1 small (or ½ large) red cabbage, finely shredded
¼ cup water

Wash the leeks well and slice finely. Heat the oil and butter together in a frying pan over medium heat, add the leek, bacon and onion, and sauté until the onion is transparent. Add the cabbage and water. Stir to combine. Reduce the heat to low, place a lid on the pot and gently braise for 20 minutes. Remove the lid and cook for a few minutes more if necessary to evaporate off any excess liquid.

Parsnip Mash
Serves 6

600g parsnips, peeled
¾ cup water
60g butter

Remove the tough core from the parsnips and place in a saucepan. Add the water. Bring to the boil and then simmer until the parsnips are very tender. Drain then whisk in the butter and salt and pepper to taste.

HOPPEL POPPEL

Serves 4

This American breakfast dish is one I make often. It is particularly useful for using up leftover toppings from making a pizza; salami is particularly good, but leftover **roast pork** can be added instead or as well. And, of course, it can be served any time of day.

> 2 teaspoons olive oil
> 1 cup chopped salami*
> 1 onion, finely diced
> 1 capsicum, diced
> 1 cup roughly chopped mushrooms
> 8 eggs
> ½ cup milk
> ½ teaspoon salt (optional)
> ½ cup grated tasty cheese

Heat the oven to 160°C. Grease an 18cm x 28cm lasagne dish.

Heat the oil in a frying pan over medium-high heat and sauté the salami for 3 minutes. Remove the salami with a slotted spoon and drain on absorbent kitchen paper. Discard the fat in the pan but don't wash it. Add the onion and capsicum to the pan and sauté for 3 minutes, then place in the prepared dish with the salami. Sauté the mushrooms for 3 minutes and spoon into the dish.

In a bowl whisk the eggs, milk and salt together and pour over the vegetables. Sprinkle on the cheese, then mix together until well combined.

Bake for 30 minutes, or until set.

* *If using leftover meat other than salami, there is no need to sauté it, rather, simply add it with the cheese and mix through.*

SPICY PORK OR LAMB TRIANGLES

Makes 8

1 tablespoon olive oil
1 small onion, peeled and finely diced
150g cooked roast pork or lamb, minced or very finely diced
1 spring onion, finely sliced (optional)
30g cream cheese or ricotta
1 teaspoon paprika
1 teaspoon ground cumin
½ teaspoon ground coriander
½ teaspoon finely grated lemon rind
pinch of ground fennel seeds (optional)
2 teaspoons sweet chilli sauce
1 tablespoon Greek or plain yoghurt
2 teaspoons lemon juice
½ cup grated tasty cheese
2 sheets frozen puff pastry, thawed
30g butter, cut into 8 pieces
3 tablespoons (approximately) milk

Heat the oven to 200°C. Line 2 baking trays with baking paper.

Heat the oil in a frying pan over medium heat and sauté the onion until
transparent. Remove the pan to cool. Stir in the pork or lamb, spring onion,
cream cheese, paprika, cumin, coriander, lemon rind, fennel (if using), chilli
sauce, yoghurt, lemon juice, cheese and salt to taste. Mix well.

Cut each pastry sheet into 4 squares. Divide the meat mixture among the
squares, top each with 1 piece of the butter, dampen 2 edges of each
pastry, then fold diagonally over to form triangles. Brush with the milk and
prick once with a fork. Bake for 5 minutes, then reduce the heat to 170°C
and bake for 20 minutes more, or until the pastry is crispy and golden.

Serve with sour cream and sweet chilli sauce.

Sausages and Rissoles

After a barbecue or even a sausage sizzle, there are few things sadder than a pile of sausages sitting cold and shrivelled on a plate. The following recipes rehydrate and invigorate them to make new meals with a minimum of effort.

◆

CREAMY CURRIED SAUSAGES

Serves 4–6

300g (approximately) cooked sausages
30g butter
2 teaspoons curry powder
2 teaspoons chicken stock powder
3 cups milk
1½ tablespoons cornflour mixed to a paste with ¼ cup of milk
2 teaspoons tomato sauce (ketchup)
½ cup grated tasty cheese

Cut the sausages into 2cm lengths.

In a large saucepan melt the butter over low heat, add the curry powder and stock powder and sauté for 1 minute. Add the milk and bring barely to a boil. Thicken by mixing in some or all of the cornflour paste, stirring until it thickens, then mix in the tomato sauce and grated cheese and stir until melted.

Add the sausages and simmer for 2 minutes. Add salt and pepper to taste.

Serve with plain boiled or steamed rice and seasonal vegetables or salad.

SAVOURY SAUSAGES

Serves 4–6

350g (approximately) cooked sausages
2 tablespoons olive oil
1 onion, diced
1 carrot, diced
1 stick celery, sliced
½ parsnip, diced (optional)
2 teaspoons curry powder or curry paste
1 dessertspoon chutney
1 dessertspoon tomato sauce (ketchup)
1 dessertspoon soy sauce
1 dessertspoon Worcestershire sauce
1 dessertspoon sweet chilli sauce
1 teaspoon brown sugar or seedless jam
400g tin diced tomatoes
1 cup chicken stock or water
1½ tablespoons cornflour mixed to a paste with ¼ cup of cold
    water

Cut the sausages into 1cm lengths.

Heat the oil in a saucepan over medium-high heat and add the vegetables.
Sauté until almost tender, then add curry powder and cook for 1 minute
more. Add the chutney, sauces, sugar or jam, tomatoes and stock or water.

Bring to the boil, then simmer for 15 minutes. Add the sausage pieces and
simmer for 5 minutes more. If it needs to be thickened, stir in some or all
of the cornflour paste, stirring until it thickens, then add salt and pepper
to taste.

Serve with plain boiled or steamed rice and seasonal vegetables or salad.

TOAD IN A HOLE

Serves 4

This recipe is good for using up cooked sausages, but it can really be applied to any type of leftover cooked meat. The addition of herbs to the batter is optional, but it naturally gives greater flavour. For instance, I would add rosemary if using lamb sausages, fennel for pork and parsley with spring onions for beef.

It is best to use a metal tin to make toad in a hole as it allows for faster cooking and optimum rising of the batter.

> **4–6 leftover cooked sausages or about 500g cooked steak,**
> **chops or hamburgers, cubed**
> 2 eggs
> 1 cup milk
> 1 cup plain flour
> 1 teaspoon baking powder
> ½ teaspoon salt
> 1–2 tablespoons chopped fresh herbs (optional)

Heat the oven to 200°C. Grease a 20cm square or round tin.

Cut each sausage crossways into quarters and place in the prepared tin.

In a bowl beat together the eggs, milk, flour, baking powder, salt and herbs until very well combined. Pour over the sausages.

Bake in the oven for 10 minutes, then reduce heat to 160°C and bake for 10–15 minutes more, or until the batter is well risen and golden.

Serve with chutney and salad or seasonal vegetables.

SAUSAGES IN ONION GRAVY

Serves 4

2 tablespoons olive oil
2 teaspoons butter
3 onions, finely sliced*
1¼ cups chicken stock, or water with 1 teaspoon stock
     powder
1 tablespoon tomato sauce (ketchup)
2 teaspoons cornflour mixed to a paste with ¼ cup of water
4–6 cooked sausages

Heat the oil and butter in a saucepan over medium-high heat until the butter is melted. Reduce heat and sauté the onions until tender and golden brown. Stir in the stock and tomato sauce and bring to the boil. Simmer for 5 minutes, then to thicken whisk in some or all of the cornflour paste, stirring until it thickens.

Leave the sausages whole or cut them into pieces and add to the gravy. Simmer gently for 3 minutes, or until the sausages are heated through. Add salt and pepper to taste.

Serve with creamy mashed potatoes.

* *If you have leftover cooked onions from the barbecue, use about 1 cup of these in place of the raw onions and sauté gently for 2 minutes.*

Spaghetti and meatballs

Serves 4

After a barbecue there may be leftover rissoles which can be turned into meatballs for this recipe. If you prefer, you could make the tomato sauce and reheat the rissoles and serve with mashed potatoes and seasonal vegetables instead of with spaghetti.

1 tablespoon olive oil
125g lean bacon, diced
1 red capsicum, diced
1 onion, finely diced
2 cups chopped tomatoes, fresh, bottled or tinned
2 tablespoons tomato paste
1 dessertspoon soy sauce
1 dessertspoon Worcestershire sauce
2 teaspoons sweet chilli sauce
3 teaspoons chutney (any sort)
1 cup beef, chicken or vegetable stock
6–8 leftover patties or rissoles
3 tablespoons freshly grated parmesan cheese
1 x 500g packet spaghetti or fettuccini

Heat the oil in a saucepan over medium heat and sauté the bacon, capsicum and onion until the onion is transparent. Add the tomatoes, tomato paste, sauces, chutney and stock. Bring to the boil and simmer for 20 minutes.

Cut the rissoles into 4 pieces and add to the sauce. Simmer for 3 minutes, or until the meat is heated through. Add salt and pepper to taste.

Cook the spaghetti or fettuccini according to the directions on the packet. Serve topped with the meatballs and parmesan sprinkled on top.

Ham

Certainly at Christmas time and often other times, there is leftover ham in the fridge. As well as the recipes to follow, leftover ham can make a tasty addition to many dishes such as: a topping for pizzas, scrambled eggs or quiches, casseroles, fried rice, or pasta sauces.

◆

Ham, Chicken and Asparagus Pie

Serves 4−6

500g skinless chicken thigh or breast fillets, diced
1 tablespoon oil
1 onion, finely diced
1 stick celery, finely diced
1 carrot, finely diced
2 cloves garlic, crushed
1 rounded tablespoon Dijon mustard
2 teaspoons chopped fresh thyme (or ¼ teaspoon dried thyme)
1 cup (approximately) diced ham
¾ cup milk
1 tablespoon lemon juice
1 teaspoon chicken or vegetable stock powder
1 tablespoon whole-egg mayonnaise
3 teaspoons cornflour mixed to a paste with 2 tablespoons of cold water
1 cup (approximately) drained tinned asparagus cuts*
1 sheet frozen puff pastry, thawed

Heat the oven to 200°C. Grease a 20cm casserole dish.

Heat the oil in a saucepan over medium heat. Add the chicken, onion, celery, carrot and garlic and sauté until the chicken has completely changed colour and is almost cooked through. Add the mustard, thyme, ham, milk, lemon juice, stock powder and mayonnaise. Bring to the boil, then if it needs to be thickened, whisk in some or all of the cornflour paste, stirring until it thickens. Fold in the asparagus.

Pour into the prepared casserole dish and top with the pastry. Prick in several places.

Bake for 10 minutes, then reduce heat to 170°C and cook for a further 10 minutes, or until the pastry is well risen and golden brown.

Serve with fresh seasonal vegetables.

* *Cooked fresh asparagus, cut into 1 cm lengths, can be substituted for the tinned variety.*

RICH BEEF HOTPOT

Serves 4

2 tablespoons olive oil
600g lean cubed stewing beef (such as blade, chuck or
    topside)
1 cup leftover ham, cut into strips or 1cm cubes
1 large onion, diced
1 red capsicum, diced
2 garlic, crushed
⅓ cup red wine
2 cups beef stock
2 tablespoons tomato sauce (ketchup)
1 tablespoon Worcestershire sauce
2 teaspoons chopped fresh thyme leaves
2 bay leaves
½ teaspoon salt
¼ teaspoon ground black pepper
3 teaspoons cornflour mixed to a paste with 2 tablespoons of
    cold water

Heat the oil in a large saucepan over high heat and sauté the beef until well coloured. Add the ham, onion and capsicum and sauté for 5 minutes more, then add the garlic and sauté for a further minute. Stir in the wine and cook for 1 minute, then add the stock, sauces, thyme and bay leaves, salt and pepper.

Bring to the boil and simmer for 1½–2 hours or until the beef is tender. Stir in some or all of the cornflour paste, stirring until it thickens.

Serve with fresh seasonal vegetables.

HAM AND CHEESE SCROLL

Serves 4

This scroll is delicious sliced and served with soup.

>2 cups self-raising flour
>½ teaspoon mustard powder
>¼ teaspoon salt
>2 tablespoons butter
>1½ cups grated cheese
>½–¾ cup milk
>**½–1 cup chopped leftover ham**
>1 small egg, lightly whisked
>1–2 tablespoons sesame seeds

Heat the oven to 190°C. Grease a baking tray or line with baking paper.

In a bowl combine the flour, mustard and salt. Add the butter and half of the cheese and rub in with the fingertips until the mixture resembles coarse breadcrumbs.

Add the milk and mix to a firm dough.

Roll out the dough on a lightly floured board to 1cm thick. Sprinkle with the remaining cheese and chopped ham.

Roll up from long side as for a Swiss Roll. Place on the prepared tray and make shallow cuts 1cm apart across the roll. Brush with the egg and sprinkle with sesame seeds.

Bake for 20 minutes until well risen and golden.

Remove to a wire rack to cool completely.

VARIATION

¼ cup chopped semi-dried tomatoes can be also added to the filling.

HAM AND ZUCCHINI SLICE

Serves 6—8

The slice can be cut into small pieces for young children. It is easy to handle, tasty and nutritious.

> 375g zucchini, grated
> 1 onion, grated or finely diced
> 1 red capsicum, finely diced
> 1 cup creamed corn (optional)
> **1–2 cups diced leftover ham**
> 1 cup grated tasty cheese
> ½ cup light olive oil
> 6 eggs
> ½ teaspoon salt
> 2 tomatoes, sliced

Heat the oven to 170°C. Grease an 18cm x 28cm x 3cm slab tin.

In a bowl mix all the ingredients together except for the tomatoes, then pour into the prepared tin. Place the sliced tomatoes decoratively over the top and sprinkle with a little salt and pepper.

Bake in a moderate oven for 30–40 minutes or until set.

Serve with a green salad.

HAM AND CHEESE MINI MUFFINS

Makes 12

These little muffins make an ideal after-school snack for children.

> 1½ cups self-raising flour
> 1 egg
> ½ cup milk
> 2 tablespoons butter, melted
> **4 tablespoons chopped leftover ham**
> 2 tablespoons chopped parsley
> **½ cup grated tasty cheese scraps**
> 1 tablespoon chopped chives or spring onion tops (optional)

Heat the oven to 200°C. Line 12 x ¼-cup capacity muffin tins with paper cases.

Put the flour into a large mixing bowl.

In another bowl, whisk the egg well and add the milk. Add this mixture and the butter to the flour.

Using a metal spoon, fold together until the mixture is just combined.

Add the ham, parsley, cheese and chives or onion (if using), and fold through until all the ingredients are well combined

Spoon the mixture evenly into the paper cases. Bake for 15 minutes or until a skewer inserted into the centre comes out clean.

Remove the muffins from the muffin tins but leave them in the paper cases and cool on a wire rack.

Store in an airtight container in the fridge for up to 3 days.

DAIRY

Small leftover pieces of butter can go neglected in the fridge and may go rancid. Instead, wrap them in cling film and freeze for up to one month.

Cheese scraps can be frozen. The texture becomes a bit crumbly but they can still be used in sauces. Cream cheese does not freeze well.

Cream, pouring or thickened, can be frozen for later use (up to one month). The consistency will alter, but it still whips well and can be added to soups and creamy pasta sauces. Sour cream does not freeze well.

Leftover amounts of yoghurt can be used in most baking recipes in place of milk. If you only have a very little make up the quantity with milk.

CHEESE

(See also Ham and Cheese Mini Muffins, page 112.)

If some cheese looks as if it's going to waste, it's a good idea to use it up quickly as mouldy cheese can be quite dangerous to eat. It can be frozen of course, but if frozen in its block form, I find it tends to dry out and be crumbly. It is one of the most versatile of ingredients however, as the following recipes indicate.

CHEESE-FILLED RISSOLES

Serves 4

600g best minced beef
¾ cup fresh breadcrumbs
½ teaspoon salt
1 egg, lightly whisked
2 teaspoons chutney
2 teaspoons soy sauce
2 teaspoons Worcestershire sauce
1 onion, finely chopped or grated
½ **cup diced cheese scraps**
3 tablespoons oil for shallow frying

Mix together all the ingredients, except for the cheese and oil, and shape into rissoles. Flatten out each rissole in the palm of your hand and place a piece of cheese in the centre, then wrap the rissole mixture around the cheese, being careful to enclose it completely.

Heat the oil in a frying pan over medium heat. Cook the rissoles for 3 minutes on one side, turn and cook for approximately 3 minutes on the other side, or until the rissoles are cooked through.

Serve with gravy, tomato sauce or chutney and seasonal vegetables.

Sauces and Spreads

Cheese Sauce
Makes about 1½ cups

This cheese sauce has a range of uses, for example as a sauce for cauliflower or as the cheese sauce for a lasagne.

1½ cups milk
3 teaspoons cornflour mixed to a paste with 2 tablespoons of
    cold milk
60g cheese scraps, finely diced or grated
¼ teaspoon salt

Heat the milk in a medium saucepan, and when just boiling whisk in the cornflour paste, stirring until it thickens. Add the cheese and stir until melted. Add the salt and white pepper to taste.

Curry Sauce
Makes about 1 cup

This basic curry sauce can be added to leftover fish, chicken, vegetables or chopped hard boiled eggs.

30g butter
1 teaspoon curry powder
1 rounded tablespoon flour
1 cup milk
60g cheese scraps, finely diced or grated
¼ teaspoon salt

Melt the butter in a saucepan over a low heat and sauté the curry powder for 1 minute, or until fragrant. Mix in the flour and cook, stirring constantly, for 1 minute. Gradually add the milk while stirring constantly so lumps don't form. Keep stirring until it boils and thickens. Add the cheese and stir until melted. Add the salt.

Cheese Spread
Makes about ⅔ cup

This spread can be used as a topping on biscuits or mini bruschettas (page 12), or as a filling for sandwiches where, for example, it can be used instead of butter. This recipe can be doubled.

125g cheese scraps, diced
30g butter, diced
1 teaspoon dry sherry (optional)
1 teaspoon lemon juice
½ teaspoon Dijon or ¼ teaspoon hot English mustard
30g melted butter, extra

Place all the ingredients, except for the extra butter, in a bowl and place over simmering water (do not allow the water to touch the base of the bowl). Whisk or stir until the mixture has melted and is smooth. Pour into small jars and cover with the extra melted butter.

CORNED SILVERSIDE OF BEEF WITH PARSLEY DIJONNAISE SAUCE

Serves 4–6

1.5–2kg piece corned silverside of beef
1 onion, peeled and chopped in half
1 tablespoon whole cloves
1 teaspoon mixed spice or allspice berries
1 tablespoon peppercorns
1 tablespoon brown sugar
1 tablespoon vinegar, any type
1½ cups milk
2 rounded teaspoons cornflour mixed to a paste with
    2 tablespoons of cold milk
½ cup grated or finely diced cheese scraps
½ teaspoon hot English mustard
2 teaspoons lemon juice
2 tablespoons chopped parsley

Place silverside in a large pot, together with the onion, cloves, mixed spice or allspice berries, peppercorns, brown sugar and vinegar, and pour in enough cold water to cover the meat.

Bring to the boil and simmer for 1½–2 hours, or until the beef is just tender.

Heat the milk until just boiling and whisk in the cornflour paste, stirring until thickened. Add the cheese and stir over low heat until melted. Add the mustard, lemon juice, parsley and salt and white pepper to taste.

Slice the meat and serve drizzled with the sauce and seasonal vegetables.

APPLE PIE WITH LEMON CHEESE PASTRY

Serves 6

125g butter
125g sugar
1 teaspoon finely grated lemon rind
1 egg
30g custard powder or cornflour
220g plain flour
1½ teaspoons baking powder
2 tablespoons finely grated cheese
1½ cups cold stewed apple

In a bowl mix together the butter, sugar and lemon rind until creamy and light. Whisk in the egg.

Sift together the custard powder or cornflour, plain flour and baking powder. Fold into the egg mixture together with the cheese and mix until a soft dough is formed. Wrap the dough in cling wrap and refrigerate for 30 minutes at least.

Heat the oven to 200°C. Grease a 20cm pie dish.

Roll out two thirds of the pastry on a lightly floured surface to about 3mm thickness and line the base and sides of the pie dish. Spoon the stewed apple, sweetened to taste if desired, into the pie dish. Dampen the edge of the pastry with a little water. Roll out the remaining third of the pastry, place over the top of the apple and press the 2 pastry edges together. Prick the top with a fork in several places.

Bake in the oven for 10 minutes, then reduce the heat to 160°C and bake for a further 20 minutes, or until the pastry is crisp and golden.

CREAM CHEESE ICE CREAM

Makes about 700ml

90g cream cheese, softened
2 teaspoons golden syrup
¾ cup icing sugar
¼ teaspoon vanilla extract or essence
375ml tin evaporated milk, chilled overnight

In a bowl whisk together the cream cheese, golden syrup, icing sugar and vanilla until smooth.

In a separate large bowl, beat the evaporated milk with an electric beater until thick and creamy. With the beaters still running, gradually add the cream cheese mixture. Pour into ice cream trays, cover the surface with cling wrap and freeze until firm.

Hint: *Remove ice cream from freezer a few minutes before serving to allow it to soften a little.*

MARMALADE AND COTTAGE CHEESE HOTCAKES

Makes 6 hotcakes or 12 pikelets

These delicious hotcakes are wonderful served at breakfast.

    1 cup self-raising flour
    1 teaspoon baking powder
    ¾ cup milk
    2 teaspoons lemon juice
    1 egg
    1½ tablespoons marmalade
    1 tablespoon cottage cheese

In a bowl whisk together the flour, baking powder, milk, lemon juice and egg until smooth. Fold in the marmalade and cottage cheese.

Grease a frying pan with butter or spray with cooking oil and heat over medium heat.

Place approximately 1½ tablespoonfuls of the mixture in the pan, allowing room for a little spreading. Cook until bubbles begin to appear on the top and the bottom is golden, then flip over and cook for 2 minutes more, or until the other side is brown and the hotcake is cooked through.

For pikelet size, place only ¾ tablespoonfuls of the mixture in the pan and then cook as for hotcakes.

Serve with fresh or stewed fruit or spread with a little honey.

CREAM AND SOUR CREAM

Cream can be frozen for later use but its texture will not be quite the same, however it will be perfectly fine for whipping and cooking. Sour cream does not freeze well.

CHEESY CREAMED SPINACH

Makes about 3 cups

8 spinach or silver beet leaves
2 tablespoons water
1½ cups milk
½ teaspoon salt
3 teaspoons cornflour
90g grated tasty cheese
1 tablespoon sour cream

Wash the spinach or silver beet, remove the stalks and shred finely. Place in a saucepan with the water. Bring to the boil and simmer for 3 minutes. Drain well.

Place the spinach back in the saucepan with 1¼ cups of the milk and salt. Bring to the boil and remove from heat.

Mix the cornflour with the remaining ¼ cup of milk and stir into the spinach mixture. Cook while stirring until it thickens.

Add the grated cheese and stir until melted, then stir in the sour cream. Add salt and white pepper to taste.

Serve as an accompaniment to fish or chicken, or as a stand-alone vegetarian dish.

EASY FAIL-PROOF SCONES

Makes 12 large scones

3 cups self-raising flour
1 teaspoon baking powder
1 teaspoon icing sugar
pinch of salt
½ cup cream
½ cup milk
1 cup water
lightly beaten egg or milk for glazing

Heat the oven to 180°C. Grease an 18cm x 28cm tray and line the base with baking paper.

In a large bowl mix together the flour, baking powder, icing sugar and salt. Make a well in the centre. Pour in the cream, milk and water and mix together until a soft dough is formed.

Turn out onto a lightly floured bench and shape into a rectangle about 2cm thick.

Using a scone cutter that has been dipped in flour, cut out the scones and place them on the prepared tray side by side with no space between them. Butting up against one another helps to prevent them from leaning sideways as they cook.

Glaze the top of the scones with a little lightly beaten egg or milk, if desired.

Bake for 20 minutes, or until well risen and golden.

Serve with jam and sweetened whipped cream.

VARIATION

For fruit scones, add 1 cup of chopped dates or other dried fruits, along with 1½ teaspoons of ground cinnamon.

Hint: *For crisp-crust scones, immediately turn the scones out onto a wire rack to cool. For soft-crust scones, line a large bowl with a tea towel and place the warm scones in this and cover loosely with another tea towel.*

WHIPPED CREAM CAKE

Serves 6–8

1 cup pouring or thickened cream
2 eggs
1 cup sugar
2 teaspoons lemon juice
1½ cups self-raising flour
⅓ cup raspberry jam
2 teaspoons icing sugar

Heat the oven to 170°C. Grease a 20cm round cake tin, line the base with baking paper, and grease again.

In a bowl whisk the cream until slightly thickened. In another bowl beat the eggs and sugar together until light and fluffy, then mix in the cream and lemon juice. Fold in the flour. Pour into the prepared cake tin and bake for 30 minutes, or until a metal skewer inserted into the centre comes out clean.

Allow to stand in the tin for 5 minutes, then turn out onto a wire rack and invert the right way up. Allow to cool completely.

Cut the cake in half crossways and spread the base with the raspberry jam. Top with the other half of the cake. Sift the icing sugar over the top.

YOGHURT

YOGHURT BREAD

Makes 1 loaf

Because of the addition of yoghurt, this bread has a hint of the flavour of sourdough.

> 3 cups plain flour
> 1 cup wholemeal plain flour
> 2 tablespoons rye flour (optional)
> 4 teaspoons dried yeast
> 3 teaspoons sugar
> 2 teaspoons salt
> 3 teaspoons olive oil
> **2 tablespoons plain or Greek yoghurt**
> 1¾ cups (approximately) warm water
> lightly beaten egg for brushing (optional)

In a large bowl, mix together the flours, yeast, sugar and salt. Make a well in the centre and pour in the oil, yoghurt and warm water. Mix together, adding extra water if necessary to make a soft dough. Sprinkle just a little extra flour over the top of the dough, cover with a tea towel and leave it to rise for 50 minutes, or until approximately doubled in size.

Line a baking tray with baking paper.

Turn the dough out onto a lightly floured surface, dust with flour and knead for about 5 minutes until the dough is smooth. Shape into a Vienna-style loaf and place on the prepared tray. Leave it to rise at room temperature for 20 minutes.

In the meantime heat the oven to 200°C.

When the oven has heated, carefully slash the top of the dough to a depth of 3mm at 1.5cm intervals. Brush with the egg if you want a really golden crust.

Bake for 30 minutes, or until it sounds hollow when tapped with a finger nail. Remove from the oven and transfer to a wire rack to cool.

RAITA

Makes about 1 ½ cups

½ Lebanese or telegraph cucumber
¼ teaspoon salt
pinch of ground coriander
2 teaspoons finely chopped spring onion top, or 2 teaspoons
   grated onion
½ cup plain or Greek yoghurt

Remove and discard the seeds from the cucumber and coarsely grate. Place in a colander and mix the salt through. Leave to stand for 30 minutes. After this time, place the cucumber in a tea towel and wring out any liquid.

Mix the cucumber with the rest of the ingredients.

Serve with curries or Spicy Pork or Lamb Triangles (page 101).

NAAN BREADS

Serves 4–6

2 cups plain flour
2 teaspoons dried yeast
1 teaspoon sugar
1 teaspoon salt
1 teaspoon baking powder
½ teaspoon bicarbonate of soda
½ cup warm milk
½ cup **plain or Greek yoghurt**
1 egg
2 teaspoons olive oil
2 teaspoons lemon juice

Mix the flour, yeast, sugar, salt, baking powder and bicarbonate of soda in a medium-sized mixing bowl and combine well.

Whisk together the milk, yoghurt, egg, olive oil and lemon juice. Pour into the dry mixture and stir until well combined, adding a little warm water if necessary to make a soft dough. Cover with a tea towel and leave in a warm place to rise until doubled in size.

Heat the oven to 200°C. Grease 3 x 30cm square baking trays, or line with baking paper.

Turn the dough out onto a lightly floured bench and knead for 2–3 minutes or until smooth. Cut the dough into 4–6 pieces and dust each lightly with flour. Roll out each piece to an oval 12–15cm long and 8–10cm wide. Place on the prepared trays and leave to rise for 20 minutes.

Bake for 10–15 minutes.

Serve immediately or remove to wire racks to cool.

Butter Chicken

Serves 4–6

Marinade
½ cup plain, Greek or seedless fruit yoghurt
2 teaspoons olive oil
1 teaspoon cornflour
½ teaspoon dried chilli flakes (optional)
1 teaspoon ground turmeric
2 teaspoons ground cumin
1 teaspoon ground cardamom
1½ teaspoons ground coriander
2 teaspoons paprika
1 tablespoon lime or lemon juice
1 teaspoon salt
2 teaspoons crushed garlic
1 tablespoon grated green ginger root
¼ teaspoon finely grated lemon rind

600g diced skinless chicken, diced
1 tablespoon peanut or olive oil
1 leek, white part only, diced
1 small onion, diced
1 red capsicum, diced
1 teaspoon ground cumin
2 tablespoons tomato paste
1 tablespoon chutney (any sort)
1 teaspoon brown sugar or seedless jam
½ cup chicken or vegetable stock or water
1 tablespoon sweet chilli sauce
¼ cup cream or coconut cream

To make the marinade, place all the marinade ingredients in a bowl and stir well to combine. Add the chicken and thoroughly coat in the marinade. Leave to marinate for 2 hours at least, if possible.

Drain the chicken, reserving the marinade.

Heat the oil in a large frying pan or wok and sauté the leek, onion and capsicum until the onion is transparent. Add the chicken and sauté for 5 minutes more. Add the cumin, tomato paste, chutney, sugar, stock, sweet chilli sauce and the reserved marinade. Simmer for 5 minutes, then stir in the cream. Reheat but do not boil.

Serve over couscous or boiled or steamed rice with Raita (page 125). An especially good accompaniment is Naan Breads (page 126).

GARLIC MASHED POTATOES

Serves 4–6

The garlic in this recipe makes for a very tasty mash. If you would prefer a rounder flavour with less 'punch' from the garlic, roast the garlic clove until soft first.

> 600g potatoes
> 30g butter
> 1 clove garlic, peeled and crushed
> ¼–⅓ **cup plain or Greek yoghurt**
> ½ teaspoon salt (or to taste)

Peel the potatoes and cut into 2.5cm cubes. Cook in boiling salted water until very tender or steam them. Drain and mash the potatoes until very smooth. Whisk in the butter, garlic, yoghurt and salt, adding extra salt if liked.

ORANGE CAKE WITH SPICED GRAND MARNIER SAUCE

Serves 8

Cake
180g butter
1½ cups sugar
2 eggs
finely grated rind of 2 large oranges
½ cup plain yoghurt
½ cup orange juice
2 cups self-raising flour

Syrup
250g sugar
½ cup strained orange juice
½ cup water
2 tablespoons lemon juice
1 piece star anise
1 cinnamon stick
6 whole cloves
½ teaspoon butter
1 tablespoon Grand Marnier or brandy

Heat the oven to 160°C. Grease a 23cm round cake tin, line the base with baking paper, and grease again.

To make the cake, cream the butter and sugar until light and fluffy, then whisk in the eggs. Stir in the orange rind, yoghurt and orange juice and then fold in the flour, mixing with a metal spoon until smooth. Pour evenly into the prepared cake tin.

Bake for 50–60 minutes or until a skewer inserted into the centre comes out clean. Allow to stand in the tin for 10 minutes, then turn out onto a wire rack to cool completely.

To make the sauce, place all the ingredients except for the Grand Marnier in a small saucepan and bring to the boil, stirring often, then reduce the heat and simmer for 5 minutes. Stir in the Grand Marnier or brandy. Leave to cool, then strain out the spices.

Serve the cake drizzled with the syrup and a little mascarpone or whipped cream.

CHOC CHIP AND ORANGE COOKIES

Makes about 24

125g butter
¾ cup brown sugar, firmly packed
2 eggs, lightly whisked
½ cup **yoghurt, any sort**
2 teaspoons finely grated orange rind
1½ cups self-raising flour
1½ cups choc chips

Heat the oven to 150°C. Line 3 baking trays with baking paper.

In a bowl cream the butter and sugar together. Whisk in the eggs, yoghurt and orange rind, then with a metal spoon mix in the flour and choc chips.

Place teaspoonfuls of mixture on the trays and bake for 12–15 minutes, or until light golden. Cool on wire racks.

Store in an airtight container for up to 1 week.

PEAR AND CINNAMON TART

Makes 12 squares

This slice is delicious served as a dessert with sweetened whipped cream, yoghurt, ice cream or Egg Yolk Custard (page 144). Any leftovers can be used as an afternoon tea cake or lunchbox treat.

1 egg
¾ cup sugar
2 tablespoons lemon juice
2 tablespoons yoghurt, any sort
¼ cup milk
60g butter, melted
1½ cups self-raising flour
3 pears
1 tablespoon melted butter, extra
½ teaspoon ground cinnamon
1 tablespoon sugar, extra

Heat the oven to 160°C. Grease an 18cm x 28cm lamington tin.

Whisk the egg and sugar together in a bowl until well combined. Add the lemon juice, yoghurt, milk, flour and butter all at once, and mix to a smooth batter. Spoon into the prepared tin and spread out to smoothly cover the base of the tin. If this is difficult to do, smooth out with the back of a spoon that has been dipped in hot water.

Peel and core the pears and cut into quarters. Cut each quarter into 3 pieces. Place decoratively over the cake batter.

Bake for 30 minutes or until a metal skewer inserted into the centre comes out clean.

Immediately brush the surface with the extra melted butter and sprinkle with the cinnamon and extra sugar. Cool in the tin.

WATERMELON SHERBET

Serves 3–4

This sherbert is delicious as a dessert or as a palate cleanser between courses of a meal.

½ cup sugar
½ cup water
450g diced watermelon flesh, seeds removed
juice of 1 small lime
juice of ½ lemon
¼ cup plain, Greek or berry yoghurt

Place the sugar and water in a small saucepan and bring to the boil, stirring often. Remove from the heat and cool.

Place the watermelon, lime and lemon juice and yoghurt in the bowl of a food processor and purée until smooth. Mix in the cooled sugar syrup. Pour into a container and freeze.

To serve, scrape the sherbet out of the container with a spoon, granita-style, and serve immediately in decorative stemmed glasses.

Yoghurt and Rhubarb Cake

Serves 6—8

125g butter
1½ cups caster sugar
1 egg
1 cup plain flour
1 cup self-raising flour
1 teaspoon vanilla extract or essence
¾ cup milk
2 tablespoons plain or Greek yoghurt
2 cups diced rhubarb
1 tablespoon cornflour

Topping
¾ cup lightly packed brown sugar
2 teaspoons ground cinnamon
2 tablespoons self-raising flour
60g butter, diced

Heat the oven to 180°C. Grease a 20cm round cake tin, line the base with baking paper, and grease again.

Cream the butter and sugar in a bowl, then whisk in the egg. Fold in the plain and self-raising flours, vanilla, milk and yoghurt, and mix with a metal spoon until well combined.

Toss the rhubarb with the cornflour and fold into the cake batter. Pour into the prepared tin.

To make the topping, combine all the ingredients in a bowl and rub together with the fingertips to form a moist crumbly mixture. Sprinkle over the top of the cake. Bake for 30–40 minutes or until a metal skewer inserted into the centre comes out clean. Leave to stand in the tin for 5 minutes, then turn out onto a wire rack to cool completely.

EGGS

If you have your own chickens or your eggs are getting to their use-by date, turn them into a dish that uses quite a few eggs. For instance, an egg and bacon pie can be made very simply by lining a 20cm tart dish with a sheet of thawed frozen puff pastry, adding about 125g of diced bacon and 6 eggs, just lightly broken with a fork. Top with another sheet of pastry or sliced tomatoes (press the edges together well if using pastry), and bake at 200°C for 10 minutes, then reduce the heat to 150°C and bake for a further 20 minutes until the filling is set. Herbs or a little shredded spinach can also be added.

Whites of eggs can be incorporated into quiches or even bread dough. Add extra egg whites, whisked, to an omelette for greater volume and very few extra kilojoules.

Yolks can be used to make Mayonnaise or Aioli (pages 140 and 141) or whisked into hot mashed potatoes for extra richness.

Hard boiled eggs are an excellent addition to a mornay-style sauce or potato salad. They can be used to make Curried Hard Boiled Eggs (page 147) or Scotch Eggs (see recipe page 149) or Stuffed Eggs (page 150).

WHITES

(See also Bubble Choc Chews, page 45.)

Leftover egg whites can be frozen in small containers for later use. Always write the number of egg whites or their weight on the freezer label.

PAVLOVA

Serves 6

This pavlova has a crisp outer crust with a delicious marshmallow centre.

3 large egg whites
1½ cups caster sugar
1 teaspoon cornflour
1 teaspoon white vinegar
2 tablespoons boiling water

Heat the oven to 130°C. Grease a 20–23cm ovenproof plate.

Place the egg whites, sugar, cornflour and vinegar in a dry bowl, then add the boiling water. Beat with an electric beater until very stiff peaks form.

Turn out the stiff mixture onto the prepared plate and shape into an 18cm round. Bake for 10 minutes, then reduce the temperature to 90°C and bake for a further 40 minutes, or until the crust is crisp.

Leave to cool on the plate. When cold, top with sweetened whipped cream and decorate with fresh seasonal fruits.

MERINGUES

Makes about 18

1 egg white
1 cup caster sugar
1 teaspoon white vinegar
1 teaspoon cornflour
1 tablespoon boiling water

Heat the oven to 120°C. Line 2 x 30cm trays with baking paper.

Place the egg white, sugar, vinegar and cornflour in a bowl, then add the boiling water. Beat with an electric beater until stiff peaks form. Spoon or pipe 9 mounds onto each of the trays.

Bake for 1 hour, or until dry.

VARIATIONS

- Pipe the meringue mixture into 3 rounds and bake until dry. The layers can then be joined with Chocolate Ganache (see page 220) and topped with sweetened whipped cream and berry fruits.

- Pipe the meringue mixture into nest shapes, and when cooked and cooled, fill with sweetened whipped cream, topped with fresh berries.

- Add a few drops of cochineal to the meringue mixture to make pretty pink meringues. Join together with sweetened whipped cream if desired.

- Sprinkle the meringue mounds with hundreds and thousands before baking.

- Dip the bases of the cooked and cooled meringues in melted dark chocolate.

STRAWBERRY SHORTCAKES

Makes 6

These lovely little shortcakes are delicious on their own or served with the strawberry coulis.

60g butter
120g sugar
¼ teaspoon vanilla extract or essence
3 egg whites
1 tablespoon milk
125g self-raising flour
200ml thickened cream
1½ teaspoons icing sugar
1 punnet strawberries, hulled
1 tablespoon strawberry jam

Strawberry Coulis
1 punnet strawberries, hulled and chopped
1 tablespoon water
1½ tablespoons (approximately) sugar

Heat the oven to 160°C. Grease 6 x ¾-cup capacity muffin tins.

Cream the butter, sugar and vanilla until light and fluffy.

In a separate bowl, beat the egg whites until firm peaks form, but are not too dry. Fold a quarter of the egg white, milk and flour into the butter mixture, and repeat, alternating, until used up. Spoon into the prepared tins and bake for 15 minutes, or until a metal skewer inserted into the centre comes out clean. Remove the cakes from the tins and cool completely on a wire rack.

In a bowl whisk the cream with the icing sugar until firm. Slice the strawberries decoratively.

Cut each cake in half and spread the bases with the strawberry jam. Spread a little cream over this, then top with some strawberry slices and cover with a little more cream. Place the other half of the shortcake on top and spread with more of the cream and decorate with the strawberry slices.

To make the strawberry coulis, place the strawberries and water in a small saucepan, bring to the boil and simmer for 5 minutes. Add the sugar to taste and stir until dissolved. Strain the mixture through a sieve and serve with the shortcakes.

RAW SUGAR AND ALMOND MERINGUES

Makes about 18

2 egg whites
1 cup raw sugar
½ cup white sugar
2 teaspoons vinegar
2 teaspoons cornflour
1 tablespoon boiling water
½ cup slivered almonds

Heat the oven to 100°C. Line 2 x 30cm square baking trays with baking paper.

In a bowl place, in the following order, the egg whites, sugars, vinegar, cornflour and boiling water. Beat with an electric mixer until stiff peaks are formed, then fold in the almonds.

Drop heaped teaspoonfuls of the mixture on the prepared trays and bake for approximately 40 minutes, or until golden and crisp.

Allow the meringues to cool on the trays, then store in an airtight container.

YOLKS

Egg yolks should not be stored for more than 2 days in the fridge, and should be covered immediately with a little cold water to stop them from drying out. Pour the water off before using. If the egg yolks have broken, this will not be possible. However, so long as only a small amount of water has been used to cover them, they can still be included in the following recipes.

MAYONNAISE

Makes about 320ml

You will need a food processor for this.

> **2 egg yolks**
> 1 tablespoon lemon juice or white wine or cider vinegar
> 1 teaspoon Dijon mustard
> ¼ teaspoon salt
> 1 cup light olive oil

Place the egg yolks in the bowl of a food processor with the lemon juice or vinegar, mustard and salt.

Process until well combined, then, with motor running, gradually add the oil in a thin stream until the mayonnaise is thick and creamy. Add extra salt if needed.

VARIATION

Add chopped fresh herbs of your choice to flavour the mayonnaise.

AIOLI

Makes about 320ml

You will need a food processor for this.

> **2 egg yolks**
> 1 clove garlic, peeled and chopped
> 1 tablespoon lemon juice or white wine vinegar
> ½ teaspoon Dijon mustard
> ½ teaspoon salt
> 1 cup light olive oil

Place the egg yolks in the bowl of a food processor with the garlic, lemon juice or vinegar, mustard and salt.

Process until well combined, then, with motor running, gradually add the oil in a thin stream until thick and creamy. Add extra salt if needed.

Aioli is especially nice simply served with chunks of fresh crusty bread.

Egg Yolk Savoury Pastry

Makes about 350g

90g butter, diced
120g plain flour
60g self-raising flour
½ teaspoon salt
1 egg yolk, lightly whisked
2 tablespoons (approximately) cold water

In a bowl rub the butter into the flours and salt with the fingertips (or use a food processor) until the mixture resembles breadcrumbs. Make a well in the centre and mix in the egg yolk and some or all of the water until a soft pastry is formed (you may need to add a little extra water).

Wrap in cling wrap and refrigerate for at least 30 minutes before using.

Egg Yolk Sweet Pastry

This pastry is ideal for sweet pies or it can be used as a biscuit dough.

Makes about 500g

125g butter
125g sugar
2 egg yolks
250g plain flour
1½ teaspoons baking powder
1 tablespoon milk

In a bowl cream the butter and sugar until light and fluffy, then whisk in the egg yolks. With a metal spoon, mix in the combined flour and baking powder, together with the milk. Wrap in cling film and place in the fridge for at least one hour before using.

Potato Swirls

Makes 12–18

> 500g potatoes, peeled and cut into chunks
> **2 egg yolks**
> ⅔ cup cream
> ¼ cup finely grated parmesan cheese
> ½ teaspoon Dijon mustard

Cook the potatoes in boiling water until tender. Drain well.

Heat the oven to 190°C. Line 2 x 30cm baking trays with baking paper.

Drain and mash the potatoes, then sieve or push through a potato ricer.

In a bowl beat egg yolks, cream, cheese and mustard until thoroughly combined. Add to the mashed potato and stir until it is well mixed and very smooth. Add salt and pepper to taste. Spoon into a piping bag fitted with a large star nozzle.

Pipe swirls onto the prepared trays.

Bake for 20 minutes or until golden brown.

Serve as an accompaniment to meat, chicken and seafood dishes.

EGG YOLK CUSTARD

Makes about 370ml

3 egg yolks
½ cup sugar
300ml milk
1 teaspoon cornflour mixed to a paste with 1 tablespoon of
    cold milk
½ teaspoon vanilla extract or essence

In a bowl whisk the egg yolks with the sugar until well combined.

Meanwhile heat the milk in a saucepan to boiling point. Pour approximately
one quarter of the hot milk into the egg yolk mixture, stirring constantly,
then pour this mixture into the remaining milk in the saucepan, together
with the cornflour paste, whisking constantly. Cook while still whisking
over a low heat until the custard thickens. Do not boil. Stir in the vanilla.

If you are not serving the custard immediately, cover the surface with cling
wrap or sprinkle with a little sugar to prevent a skin from forming.

VARIATION

Instead of the vanilla, the custard can be flavoured with 1 tablespoon of
sherry or brandy, which is very nice with a fruit pudding, such as Steamed
Fruit Pudding (page 245).

GOLDEN LEMON CAKE

Serves 6–8

3 egg yolks
1 cup sugar
¾ cup milk
¼ cup lemon juice
3 teaspoons finely grated lemon rind
1¾ cups self-raising flour
¼ cup custard powder
125g butter, melted

Lemon Icing
180g icing sugar
1 teaspoon butter, softened
1 tablespoon (approximately) lemon juice
2 teaspoons finely grated lemon rind (optional)

Heat the oven to 160°C. Grease a deep 18cm round cake tin and line the base with baking paper, then grease again.

Place all the ingredients in a large bowl and beat with an electric beater for 3 minutes, or until thick and smooth. Pour the mixture evenly into the prepared tin and bake for 40–45 minutes, or until a metal skewer inserted into the centre comes out clean. Allow to stand in the tin for 5 minutes, then turn out onto a wire rack to cool completely.

To make the icing, sift the icing sugar and add the butter. Gradually add the lemon juice until a spreadable consistency is reached, then add the lemon rind if desired. Spread over the cooked cake.

RICE CUSTARD

Serves 4

2½ cups milk
½ cup arborio rice
¼ cup sugar
½ teaspoon vanilla extract or essence
3 egg yolks
½ teaspoon ground nutmeg

Place the milk and rice in a saucepan and bring to the boil, stirring occasionally. Reduce the heat and simmer for about 20 minutes, or until the rice is tender and has absorbed the milk, stirring frequently.

Whisk together the sugar, vanilla and egg yolks, stir into the mixture and combine well. Do not allow the mixture to boil.

Serve in individual dessert bowls sprinkled with nutmeg.

HARD BOILED

CURRIED HARD BOILED EGGS

Serves 4

60g butter
2 teaspoons curry powder
1½ tablespoons flour
1½ cups milk
2 teaspoons tomato sauce (ketchup)
½ cup grated tasty cheese
4 hard boiled eggs

Melt butter in a saucepan over low heat. Add the curry powder and stir for 1 minute. Add the flour and cook for a further 2 minutes, stirring constantly.

Gradually add the milk, stirring constantly with a whisk. Bring to the boil, stirring constantly, then lower the heat and simmer for 3 minutes, still stirring.

Mix in the tomato sauce and cheese, and stir until the cheese is melted. Add salt and white pepper to taste.

Cut the eggs into quarters and carefully mix through the sauce. Place over very low heat until the eggs are heated through.

Serve with plain boiled rice.

EASY EGG AND TUNA PIE

Serves 4

This pie was a great favourite when our children were growing up – even those who didn't particularly like fish enjoyed this pie.

Well-flavoured flaked cooked fish can be substituted for the tinned tuna in this recipe, as can tinned salmon.

> 2 sheets frozen puff pastry, thawed
> 200g tin tuna in brine, drained and flaked
> 1 tablespoon chopped parsley
> 2 tablespoons lemon juice
> **4 hard boiled eggs, sliced**

Heat the oven to 200°C. Grease a 20cm square baking dish.

Place 1 sheet of pastry over the base and sides of the dish. Spread with the tuna, sprinkle with parsley, drizzle with lemon juice and top with the sliced eggs.

Dampen the edge of the pastry, place the other sheet over the top and press edges together to seal. Trim the excess. Prick in several places with a fork.

Bake for 20 minutes, or until the pastry is puffed and golden.

Serve with seasonal vegetables or green salad.

Scotch Eggs

Serves 4

Scotch eggs are nice served hot or cold.

> 250g sausage mince
> 250g best minced beef
> ½ cup fresh breadcrumbs
> 2 teaspoons tomato sauce (ketchup)
> 2 teaspoons Worcestershire sauce
> 1 teaspoon soy sauce
> ½ teaspoon salt
> **4 hard boiled eggs**
> 1 egg, lightly beaten
> 1 cup (approximately) dried breadcrumbs
> canola oil for deep frying

In a bowl combine the minces, fresh breadcrumbs, sauces and salt, and mix well. Divide into 4 and shape into flat rounds large enough to surround each egg (it is a good idea to do this on cling wrap).

Place a hard boiled egg on each round and shape the meat mixture around each egg to completely cover.

Dip in the beaten egg, then in the dried breadcrumbs. Refrigerate for 30 minutes.

Heat the oil over medium-high heat and cook scotch eggs for about 4 minutes, or until golden brown and the meat is cooked through.

Serve with fresh seasonal vegetables.

STUFFED EGGS

Serves 4

Stuffed eggs are an old-fashioned favourite that are always popular as a snack or canapé.

4 hard boiled eggs
1 tablespoon cream
2 teaspoons whole-egg mayonnaise
¼ teaspoon Dijon mustard
1 teaspoon sweet chilli sauce
1 tablespoon chopped parsley
½ cup finely grated tasty cheese

Cut the eggs in half lengthways and remove the yolks. In a bowl mash the yolks then add the rest of the ingredients and mix well, adding a little extra cream or milk if needed. Add salt and white pepper to taste.

Pipe or spoon the mixture into the cavity of the egg whites.

Tuna Mornay

Serves 4—6

You can use 3 or more hard boiled eggs in this recipe – alternatively, even just 2 is fine. Cooked fresh fish can be substituted for the tinned tuna in this recipe.

> 60g butter
> 1 small onion, peeled and very finely diced
> 2 tablespoons plain flour
> 2½ cups milk
> 2 teaspoons Dijon mustard
> 2 teaspoons whole-egg mayonnaise
> juice ½ lemon
> ½ cup grated tasty cheese
> 425g tin tuna in spring water, drained
> **3 hard boiled eggs, cut into 1cm pieces**

Melt the butter in a saucepan over low heat. Add the onion and sauté gently until transparent. Add the flour, mix well and cook for minute.

Whisk in the milk and bring to the boil, whisking constantly.

Mix in the mustard, mayonnaise and lemon juice. Simmer for about 2 minutes, or until the mixture thickens a little, stirring constantly. Add the cheese and stir until melted, the mix in the tuna and eggs. Add salt and pepper to taste.

VARIATION

To make this mixture into a pie, pour the mornay into a casserole dish and top with a sheet of thawed puff pastry or crushed cornflakes.

Bake at 200°C for 20 minutes, or until the pastry is puffed and golden.

VEGETABLES

Various pieces of fresh vegetables can be used up in soups, mornays (just sauté and add cheese sauce and tinned tuna for instance) or added to stews and other casserole-style dishes.

Leftover cooked vegetables can be added to pie fillings or to stock to make a tasty soup. They can be used in Bubble and Squeak, an old-style favourite of mashed vegetables pan fried in a little butter until browned on one side, then turned and browned on the other to a delicious crispness.

Leftover salads, depending on their nature, can be added to pasta dishes or, in the case of a green salad, simply add stock, cook for a few minutes and then puree to make a light soup.

Use the water from boiling vegetables to add to soups, stews, casseroles and gravies to give extra flavour and nutritional value.

FRESH VEGETABLES

The following two recipes are ideal for using up those bits and pieces of random vegetables that get left in the fridge crisper drawer.

QUICK CHICKEN AND VEGETABLE SOUP

Serves 4

1 tablespoon olive oil
2 teaspoons butter
4 skinless chicken thigh fillets, chopped
1 onion, chopped finely
1–3 cups diced mixed raw vegetables
440g tin creamed corn
5 cups chicken stock, or water with 3 teaspoons chicken or
    vegetable stock powder
½ teaspoon dried thyme or 3 teaspoons chopped fresh thyme

In a large saucepan, heat the oil and butter together over medium heat. Add the chicken and sauté until almost cooked through, then add the onion and vegetables and sauté for 5 minutes with the lid on over a low heat.

Add the creamed corn, chicken stock and herbs, bring to the boil and simmer for 10–15 minutes, or until the vegetables are tender. Add salt and pepper to taste.

Serve with warm crusty bread.

VEGETARIAN LASAGNE

Serves 4

2 tablespoons olive oil
1 onion, finely diced
3 cups diced mixed raw vegetables (such as carrot,
capsicum, celery, carrot, pumpkin, sweet potato)
2 cloves garlic, crushed
400g tin diced tomatoes
1 tablespoon tomato paste
3 teaspoons chutney (any sort)
2 teaspoons Worcestershire sauce
½ teaspoon salt
½ teaspoon brown sugar
½ cup beef, vegetable or chicken stock, or water
3 teaspoons chopped fresh rosemary or basil, or ½ teaspoon
dried oregano
2 teaspoons cornflour mixed to a paste with 2 tablespoons of
cold water
150g (approximately) instant lasagne sheets
1¼ cups grated tasty cheese

Cheese Sauce
1 cup milk
3 teaspoons cornflour mixed to a paste with ¼ cup of cold milk
¼ cup grated parmesan or tasty cheese
1 egg, lightly whisked

Heat the oil in a frying pan over medium-high heat and sauté the onion
and vegetables until almost tender. Add the garlic and sauté for 1 minute
more. Add the tomatoes, tomato paste, chutney, Worcestershire sauce,
salt, sugar, stock and herbs. Bring to the boil and simmer for 10 minutes.
To thicken, stir in the cornflour paste.

To make the cheese sauce, heat the milk in a small saucepan, and when boiling whisk in the cornflour paste to thicken. Stir in the parmesan until melted. Add salt and white pepper to taste. Remove from the heat and whisk in the egg.

Heat the oven to 170°C. Grease a 20cm square lasagne dish.

Pour ¾ cup of the vegetable mixture into the base, place a single layer of lasagne sheets over the top, then spread over 1½ cups of the vegetable mixture. Sprinkle with ⅓ cup of tasty cheese and cover with another layer of lasagne sheets. Spread over the remaining vegetable mixture and sprinkle with another ⅓ cup of cheese. Place another layer of lasagne sheets over the top, then pour over the cheese sauce. Sprinkle with the remaining tasty cheese.

Bake for 30 minutes until the cheese is golden brown and the lasagne sheets are tender. Allow to stand in the dish for 10–15 minutes before cutting into squares to serve.

COOKED OR PROCESSED VEGETABLES

Beetroot

♦

BEETROOT DIP

Makes 1 cup

½ cup finely grated tinned or pickled beetroot
½ cup sour cream
pinch of ground cumin
pinch of ground cloves
2 teaspoons lemon juice
¼ teaspoon salt (optional)

Mix all the ingredients together in a bowl and serve with crudités or fresh crusty bread. This is also nice served as an accompaniment to smoked salmon.

CHOCOLATE BEETROOT CUP CAKES

Makes about 24

These tasty little cakes give no hint of the flavour of their secret beetroot ingredient. Their colour is wonderful, and the flavour of the chocolate seems to be enhanced by the earthiness of the beetroot.

The recipe can be made in a 20cm round cake tin, which will take about 40 minutes to bake.

> 1 cup plain flour
> 2 tablespoons cocoa powder
> 2½ teaspoons baking powder
> ½ teaspoon bicarbonate of soda
> 2 eggs
> ½ cup sugar
> **¾ cup pureed cooked beetroot (drained tinned beetroot can be used)**
> ¾ cup light olive oil
> ½ cup dark chocolate chips, melted
>
> **Chocolate Icing**
> 30g butter, softened
> 1½ cups icing sugar
> 1½ tablespoons cocoa powder
> 2 tablespoons (approximately) boiling water
> ½ cup hundreds and thousands

Heat the oven to 170°C. Line 24 x ¼-cup capacity patty cake tins with paper cases.

In a bowl sift together the flour, cocoa, baking powder and bicarbonate of soda.

In another bowl, whisk together the eggs and sugar, then mix into the dry mixture with a metal spoon together with the beetroot, oil and chocolate, and stir until smooth. Spoon into the paper cases to two thirds full.

Bake for 12–15 minutes or until a skewer inserted into the centre comes out clean. Remove from the tins to cool on a wire rack.

To make the chocolate icing, mix the butter, icing sugar, cocoa and enough boiling water to a smooth spreadable consistency.

When the cakes are completely cold, ice them with the chocolate icing and, while the icing is still wet, sprinkle with the hundreds and thousands.

Cauliflower

◆

CAULIFLOWER CHEESE

Serves 4

1½ cups milk
3 teaspoons cornflour mixed to a paste with 2 tablespoons of
   cold milk
1 cup grated tasty cheese
¼ teaspoon salt
1 cup cooked cauliflower

Heat the oven to160°C. Grease a round or square 18cm oven proof dish.

Heat the milk in a medium saucepan. When boiling, whisk in the cornflour
paste and keep whisking until thickened. Mix in half of the cheese and stir
until melted. Add the salt and white pepper to taste. Fold in the cauliflower.

Spoon into the prepared dish, sprinkle with the remaining cheese and bake
for 15 minutes, or until the cheese is melted and the cauliflower is heated
through.

VARIATION

Substitute lightly cooked broccoli for the cauliflower.

Cauliflower Soup

Serves 2

1 tablespoon light olive oil
2 teaspoons softened butter
60g leek, white part only, finely sliced
1 cup milk
2 cups loosely packed cooked cauliflower cheese
¼ cup pouring cream or sour cream

Heat the oil and butter together in a saucepan over medium heat and gently sauté the leek until tender, then add the milk and cauliflower cheese and bring to the boil. Remove from the heat and purée. Place back on the heat and bring back to the boil, then stir in the cream but do not boil again otherwise the cream may separate. Add salt and white pepper to taste.

Serve with Pulled Bread (page 27) or Potato Rolls (page 173).

SPICY CAULIFLOWER CURRY

Serves 4 as a side dish, 2 as a main meal

2 tablespoons olive oil
1 onion, finely diced
2 cloves garlic, crushed
2 teaspoons ground cumin
1 teaspoon ground coriander
3 teaspoons chutney
1 tablespoon sweet chilli sauce
2 cups chicken or vegetable stock
4 teaspoons cornflour mixed to a paste with about
    2 tablespoons of cold water
2 cups cooked cauliflower florets
½ cup coconut cream (optional)
2 tablespoons plain yoghurt
finely chopped coriander or parsley

Heat the oil in a frying pan over medium heat. Add the onion and sauté gently until soft. Add the garlic and spices and cook for 1 minute more. Stir in the chutney, chilli sauce and stock and simmer for 10 minutes. Stir in some or all of the cornflour paste to thicken the mixture. Fold in the cauliflower and simmer for 3 minutes more until heated through. Fold in the coconut cream and yoghurt. Add salt and pepper to taste. Reheat but do not allow the mixture to boil.

Serve sprinkled with the chopped coriander or parsley.

VARIATION

- Leftover cooked peas can be added to this recipe with the cauliflower.

- Other vegetables can be used instead of cauliflower.

Kumara (sweet potato)

◆

HAMBURGER PATTIES

Serves 4—6

This recipe can also be used to make meatballs or as a filling for pasties.

600g best minced beef
1 egg, lightly whisked
1 onion, grated
½ cup cooked mashed kumara
3 slices bread, crumbed
¾ teaspoon salt
2 teaspoons chutney
2 teaspoons soy sauce
2 teaspoons Worcestershire sauce
1 tablespoon plain flour
3 tablespoons olive or canola oil for frying

Mix all the ingredients together except for the oil. Shape into hamburger patties.

Heat the oil in a heavy-based frying pan over medium-high heat. Cook the patties on one side for 4 minutes, then for 3 minutes on the other side, or until the patties are just cooked through. Drain on crumpled kitchen paper.

Serve with seasonal vegetables and tomato chutney.

KUMARA CHEESE BAKE

Serves 4

½ cup milk
250g grated tasty cheese
2 eggs, lightly beaten
2 tablespoons self-raising flour
½–¾ cup cooked mashed kumara
2 teaspoons lemon juice

Heat the oven to 160°C. Grease an 18–20cm pie or casserole dish.

Place the milk in a saucepan and bring to the boil. Remove from the heat and mix in the cheese, stirring until melted. Cool for 5 minutes.

Whisk in the eggs, then the flour, kumara and lemon juice. Add salt and pepper to taste.

Pour into the prepared dish and bake for 25 minutes, or until well risen and set.

VARIATION

Pumpkin can be substituted for Kumara.

Mushrooms

Add leftover mushrooms to a beef or chicken casserole.

◆

MUSHROOM RISOTTO

Serves 4

45g butter
1 tablespoon olive oil
1 small onion, peeled and finely diced
250g mushroom pieces (stalks or offcuts)
2 cloves garlic, peeled and finely chopped
¾ cup arborio rice
3 cups (approximately) boiling chicken stock
squeeze of lemon juice
½ cup grated parmesan cheese
½ cup grated tasty cheese
½ cup pouring cream

Melt the butter with the oil in a heavy-based frying pan over medium heat. Sauté the onion until transparent, then add the mushrooms and garlic and cook until the mushrooms release their juices.

Stir in the rice. Add 1 cup of the stock and cook until it has been absorbed by the rice, stirring frequently. Add another cup of stock and cook until absorbed, again stirring frequently. Continue this process until all the stock has been used.

Stir in the lemon juice, cheeses and cream, and add salt and white pepper to taste.

Onions

These can be included in any casserole you happen to be making. However, the following slice is very tasty indeed and makes a good luncheon dish.

◆

ONION AND RICOTTA SLICE

Serves 6

This recipe uses up leftovers (such as onions from the barbecue plate) in the tasty topping of this slice. Extra or different herbs can be added according to taste.

You could also add some chopped semi-dried tomatoes to the filling, or small pieces of roasted capsicum.

Cheese Pastry
1 cup self-raising flour
¼ teaspoon salt
45g butter
¼ cup finely grated tasty cheese
⅓ cup (approximately) milk
2 teaspoons lemon juice

Filling
2 teaspoons olive oil
125g bacon, finely diced
250g ricotta
3 eggs
1 teaspoon chopped fresh thyme
1 cup cooked onions
½ cup grated tasty cheese

Heat the oven to 200°C. Grease an 18cm x 28cm lasagne dish.

To make the pastry, mix the flour and salt together in a bowl. Add the butter and cheese and rub in with the fingertips until the mixture resembles coarse breadcrumbs. Alternatively, process to this stage in a food processor then transfer to a bowl.

Mix with a metal spoon to a soft dough with the milk and lemon juice, adding a little extra milk if necessary.

To make the filling, heat the oil in a frying pan over medium-high heat and sauté the bacon for 3 minutes. Remove the bacon and set aside.

Roll out the pastry and line the base of the prepared dish.

In a bowl whisk together the ricotta and eggs. Add the bacon, thyme and onion and mix well. Add salt and pepper to taste. Pour over the pastry. Sprinkle the cheese over the top. Bake for 10 minutes, then reduce heat to 160°C and bake for 20 minutes more, or until filling is set.

Serve with a green or Greek salad.

Potato – mashed

◆

COTTAGE PIE

Serves 4–6

1 tablespoon oil
500g minced beef
1 onion, diced
1 carrot, diced
1 stick celery, diced
1 tablespoon tomato sauce (ketchup)
3 tablespoons Worcestershire sauce
2 teaspoons soy sauce
2 teaspoons chutney, any sort
1 cup beef or chicken stock, or water
3 teaspoons cornflour mixed to a paste with a little cold
     water.
½ teaspoon salt
2 cups (approximately) mashed potato
1 egg, lightly whisked
¼ cup milk, cream or sour cream
1 cup grated tasty cheese

Heat the oven to 180°C. Grease a 20cm casserole dish.

Heat the oil in a saucepan over medium-high heat. Add the mince and
cook until well coloured, stirring often. Add the prepared vegetables and
continue to cook for a further 5 minutes.

Add the sauces, chutney and stock and simmer for 20 minutes. Add some
or all of the cornflour paste and stir until thickened. Add the salt and pepper
to taste. Pour into the prepared dish.

Whisk the potato with the egg and sour cream in a bowl until just combined, and then stir in ½ cup of the cheese. Spoon over the mince mixture and smooth out, then sprinkle with the remaining cheese.

Bake for 20 minutes or until the top is golden and the potato is heated through.

Parmesan and Potato Bake

Serves 2

300g mashed potato
2 eggs, lightly whisked
1 tablespoon self-raising flour
1 tablespoon snipped chives (optional)
50g grated parmesan cheese

Heat the oven to 170°C. Grease an 18cm pie plate or casserole dish.

Sieve the potato or push through a potato ricer. Fold in the eggs, flour, chives (if using) and parmesan until well combined. Spoon the mixture evenly into the prepared dish and bake for 20–25 minutes, or until golden.

PARSLEY AND POTATO PUFFS

Makes about 12

These tasty little puffs can be served on their own as a snack or as part of a meal. They are also nice served as a canapé with a little smoked salmon added to the mixture with the parsley.

> **375g mashed potato**
> 45g butter
> 60ml water
> 75g plain flour
> 1 egg
> 2 tablespoons finely chopped parsley
> 2 teaspoons finely grated onion
> ½ cup canola or peanut oil for frying

Sieve the potatoes or press through a potato ricer.

Melt the butter in a medium saucepan and add the water. Bring to the boil, then add the flour all at once and mix well with a wooden spoon until the mixture forms a ball.

Remove from the heat and whisk in the egg. Add the potato, parsley and onion and mix with a metal spoon until well combined.

Heat the oil in a frying pan over medium-high heat. Drop tablespoons of the mixture into the oil and cook on one side for about 3 minutes, or until golden, then turn over and brown on the other side. Drain on absorbent kitchen paper.

Potato Crisp

Serves 4—6

The crispy topping on this dish gives new life to leftover mashed potato. Instead of the crumb topping, you could use crushed cornflakes dotted with small knobs of butter, or crushed potato chips.

2 tablespoons olive oil
2 teaspoons butter
1 onion, peeled and finely diced
2 cloves garlic
2 cups mashed potato
¼ cup milk
1 egg, lightly whisked
1 tablespoon chopped parsley
½ cup grated tasty or parmesan cheese

Topping
30g butter
1 tablespoon olive oil
1½ cups fresh breadcrumbs or cornflakes
2 tablespoons finely grated parmesan cheese

Heat the oven to 170°C. Grease an 18cm x 28cm lasagne dish (or similar dish).

Heat the olive oil and butter together in a saucepan and sauté the onion until transparent, then add the garlic and cook for 1 minute more. Remove from the heat and mix in the potato, milk, egg, parsley, cheese, and salt and pepper to taste. Spoon the mixture evenly into the prepared dish.

To make the topping, heat the butter and oil together in a saucepan over medium heat, then mix in the breadcrumbs and cook until they begin to crisp. Remove from the heat and mix in the parmesan cheese. Sprinkle evenly over the potato mixture.

Bake for 30 minutes, or until topping is crunchy and the potato is heated through.

PASTIES

Makes 8

2 sheets frozen puff or shortcrust pastry*
250g minced beef
250g mashed potato
1 onion, grated
1 slice swede, grated
½ teaspoon salt
1½ teaspoons butter, cut into 8 pieces

Heat the oven to 200°C. Line 2 baking trays with baking paper.

Thaw the pastry sheets and cut into quarters.

Mix the meat, potato, onion, swede and salt.

Place approximately 1 tablespoon of the mixture on each piece of pastry and top with a piece of the butter.

Dampen 2 edges of each pastry piece. Fold the pastry diagonally over the meat mixture to enclose, pressing the edges together well, to form triangles. Prick the top once with a fork.

Bake for 10 minutes, then reduce the heat to 170°C and bake for a further 10–15 minutes, or until golden brown.

* *Instead of using frozen puff or shortcrust pastry, use the recipe for Egg Yolk Savory Pastry on page 142 to make 6 larger pasties (use a saucer as a guide to cut out circles from the rolled out pastry).*

POTATO BREAD

Makes 1 large loaf or 12–16 bread rolls

4 cups plain flour
4 teaspoons dried yeast
3 teaspoons sugar
2 teaspoons salt
1 tablespoon (approximately) mashed potato
½ cup potato water, heated to lukewarm
2 tablespoons light olive oil

Mix together the flour, yeast, sugar and salt in a large bowl. Make a well in the centre and add the mashed potato, potato water and oil and enough warm water to make a soft dough. Mix well, cover with a tea towel and leave to rise for 50 minutes, or until the dough approximately doubles in size. Turn over with a spoon and leave to rise again (this step can be done as many as 5 times).

Turn the dough out onto a floured surface and knead for a minute or two, adding more flour if necessary for easier handling.

Heat the oven to 200°C. Grease a 13cm x 21cm (approximately) loaf tin, or place a sheet of baking paper on a baking tray.

Loaf

Cut the dough in half and shape each into a ball. Place both balls in the loaf tin and allow to rise almost to the top of the tin.

Bake for 10 minutes, then reduce the heat to 170°C and bake for 25 minutes more, or until loaf sounds hollow when tapped with a finger. Turn out onto a wire rack to cool completely.

To make a Vienna-style loaf, shape the dough into an 18cm round and place it on a baking tray. Allow the dough to rise for 20 minutes, then slash the top with a sharp knife to a depth of 3mm at 1.5cm intervals.

Rolls

Cut the dough into 12–16 pieces and shape each into a ball. Place side by side on the tray. Allow to rise for 15 minutes, then bake for 15 minutes, or until golden brown.

* *Potato water is the water in which potatoes have been boiled in. If you don't have any, just use warm water.*

BOSTON BUN (WITH YEAST)

Makes 1 large round loaf

2 cups plain flour
2 teaspoons dried yeast
2 teaspoons finely grated lemon rind
2 teaspoons sugar
1 teaspoon salt
2 teaspoons ground cinnamon
1 teaspoon mixed spice
2 teaspoons marmalade or 1 tablespoon mixed peel
½ cup mashed potato
1 tablespoon oil
1 cup sultanas or mixed fruit
1 apple, peeled, cored and diced

In a large bowl mix together the flour, yeast, lemon rind, sugar, salt, cinnamon and mixed spice. Make a well in the centre and add the marmalade, mashed potato and oil. Mix into the dry ingredients, together with enough warm water to make a soft dough. Cover with a tea towel and stand in a warm spot for about 50 minutes, or until the dough approximately doubles in size.

Turn the dough out onto a surface dusted with flour. Sprinkle the dough with flour and knead for about 3 minutes or until smooth. Press out into a square 1cm thick and sprinkle the dried fruit and apple over this. Pull the dough around the fruit and knead into the dough for about 2 minutes. Shape into an 18cm round and place on a baking tray that has been lined with baking paper. Set aside to rise for 20 minutes covered loosely with a tea towel.

Heat the oven to 200°C. Bake the bun for 10 minutes, then reduce the heat to 160°C and bake for 20 minutes more. Cool on a wire rack.

If desired, when cold, ice with the following butter icing and sprinkle with ground cinnamon or desiccated coconut.

Icing
2 cups icing sugar
30g butter, softened
2 tablespoons (approximately) boiling water
a few drops cochineal (optional)
¼ cup desiccated coconut (optional)
½ teaspoon ground cinnamon (optional)

Sieve the icing sugar into a bowl and mix in the butter and enough boiling water to make a smooth spreading consistency. Add the cochineal if desired. Spread over bun and sprinkle with coconut, or, if you omit the cochineal, sprinkle with cinnamon.

BOSTON BUN (WITHOUT YEAST)

Serves 6

This loaf keeps well for several days.

> 1 cup smooth mashed potato
> 1 cup milk
> 1 cup sugar
> 1 egg, lightly whisked
> 1 cup mixed dried fruit
> 1½ teaspoons mixed spice
> 1½ teaspoons ground cinnamon
> 2 cups self-raising flour
> 2 teaspoons finely grated lemon rind
> 1 tablespoon lemon juice

Heat the oven to 170°C. Grease a deep 20cm cake tin, line the base with baking paper, and grease again.

In a large bowl whisk the potato, milk, sugar and egg together until smooth. Fold in the rest of the ingredients and mix with a metal spoon until well combined. Pour into the prepared tin and bake for 45 minutes, or until a metal skewer inserted into the centre comes out clean.

Allow to stand in the tin for 5 minutes, then turn out onto a wire rack to cool completely.

If you wish to ice the bun, use the icing recipe on the previous page.

Potato — cooked chunks or whole

◆

Chicken and Potato Salad

Serves 4

2 tomatoes
2 cups diced cooked potatoes
1 cup cooked peas
½ cup diced red onion
2 hard boiled eggs, chopped
1 stick celery, finely diced
2 tablespoons chopped parsley
2 tablespoons chopped mint
½ cup (approximately) whole-egg mayonnaise (or use
    mayonnaise from recipe on page 140)

Cut the tomato in half and scrape out the seeds. Dice the flesh finely.

In a large bowl mix together the tomato and the rest of the ingredients, adding salt and white pepper to taste.

HOT POTATO SALAD

Serves 4–6

This decadent but delicious dish makes a tasty side dish to a meal, especially a barbecue.

> **500g cooked potato chunks**
> 90g bacon, diced
> 1 onion, finely diced
> ⅓ cup cream
> ¼ cup mayonnaise
> ½ cup grated tasty cheese

Heat the oven to 180°C. Grease a 20cm casserole dish.

Cut the potatoes into 1.5cm cubes.

In a saucepan sauté the bacon and onion together until bacon begins to crisp. Remove from the heat and stir in the cream and mayonnaise and mix well. Add the cooked potato cubes and mix gently, taking care not to break the cubes. Spoon into the prepared casserole dish and sprinkle the cheese over the top.

Bake for 15–20 minutes, or until the salad is well heated through and the cheese is lightly browned.

POTATO FRITTATA

Serves 4

500g cooked potato chunks
1 tablespoon olive oil
2 teaspoons butter
1 onion, finely diced
1 rasher bacon, finely diced
2 spring onions, finely sliced
4 eggs
½ teaspoon salt
½ cup grated tasty cheese

Heat the grill to medium or heat the oven to 170°C. Grease an ovenproof frying pan.

Cut the potatoes into 1cm cubes. Heat the oil and butter together over medium-low heat in a frying pan with a heatproof handle. Add the onion and bacon and cook gently until the onion is soft. Add the potatoes and spring onion, and stir gently to combine with the onion and bacon.

Whisk the eggs and salt together in a bowl and pour over the potato mixture. Then gently fold through the cheese. Cook for about 5 minutes, or until the frittata begins to set around the edges.

Place the pan under the grill or in the oven, and cook for 15–20 minutes, or until the frittata is set.

Cut into wedges to serve.

Pumpkin

◆

PUMPKIN BREAD

Makes 1 large loaf

This recipe makes a delicious moist loaf, a good accompaniment to soups and/or cheeses. It is also nice toasted.

> 4 cups plain flour
> 4 teaspoons dried yeast
> 2 teaspoons sugar
> 2 teaspoons salt
> 1 egg
> **½ cup cooked mashed pumpkin**
> 2 teaspoons oil
> 1 cup warm water

In a large bowl mix together the flour, yeast, sugar and salt. Make a well in the centre.

In another bowl whisk together the egg, pumpkin and oil. Pour this into the well with the warm water and start to mix through the dough, adding more warm water if necessary to form a soft dough. Cover the bowl with a tea towel and leave to rise for about 1 hour, or until the dough doubles in size. Turn the dough over with a spoon and allow it to rise for another 20 minutes.

Grease 13cm x 21cm (approximately) bread tin.

Turn the dough out onto a lightly floured surface, sprinkle with flour and knead until smooth – this will take only about 3 minutes. Cut the dough in half and knead each half into a ball. Place side by side in the tin, cover with a tea towel and allow them to rise almost to the top of the tin.

Heat the oven to 200°C. Place the loaf in the oven and bake for 10 minutes, then reduce heat to 170°C and bake for 25 minutes more, or until the loaf sounds hollow when tapped with the fingertips.

Turn out onto a wire rack to cool.

PUMPKIN AND POTATO BAKE
(USING LEFTOVER PUMPKIN SOUP)

Serves 4–6

600g potatoes, peeled
1 onion, finely diced
125g bacon, finely diced
¾ cup leftover pumpkin soup
½ cup cream
½ cup grated tasty cheese

Heat the oven to 170°C. Grease a 20cm round casserole dish or 20cm square lasagne dish.

Cut the potatoes into very thin slices. Place one third of the potatoes on the base of the prepared dish, cover with half of the onion and one third of the bacon. Sprinkle with just a little salt and pepper.

In a bowl mix together the pumpkin soup and cream. Drizzle one third of the mixture over the onion and bacon. Layer another third of the potatoes, then the rest of the onion, another third of the bacon, a little salt and pepper to taste and another third of the pumpkin-cream mixture.

Top with the remaining potatoes, then the bacon, and then the remaining pumpkin-cream mixture. Sprinkle the top with the cheese.

Bake for 1 hour or until the potatoes are tender.

CORN AND PUMPKIN SOUP

Serves 4

1 tablespoon oil
2 teaspoons butter
1 leek, white part only, sliced, or 1 small onion, finely diced
2 cups cooked mashed pumpkin
400g tin creamed corn
1 cup chicken stock
1 cup milk
½ cup cream

In a large saucepan, heat the oil and butter over medium heat and sauté the leek or onion until soft. Add the pumpkin, corn, stock and milk and bring to the boil. Stir in the cream, heat through but do not boil, and add salt and pepper to taste.

Serve with fresh crusty bread.

Pumpkin and Spinach Quiche

Serves 4—6

180g spinach or silver beet, finely shredded
¼ cup water
1 sheet frozen puff pastry, thawed
3 eggs
½ cup cream
½ **cup cooked mashed pumpkin**
1 small onion, grated
200g feta, diced
½ cup grated tasty cheese
1 tomato, finely sliced
¼ teaspoon sugar

Heat the oven to 200°C. Grease a 20cm round pie dish.

In a saucepan cook the spinach or silver beet in the water over medium heat for 3 minutes, drain, cool and squeeze out the moisture.

Line the pie dish with the pastry and trim the edges.

Whisk together the eggs and cream, then stir in the pumpkin and onion. Sprinkle the feta, spinach and tasty cheese over the base of the pastry case. Pour the pumpkin mixture over. Add salt and pepper to taste. Place tomato slices decoratively on the top and sprinkle with the sugar and a little salt and pepper.

Bake for 10 minutes, then reduce the heat to 160°C and bake for another 25 minutes, or until the filling is set. Allow the quiche to stand for 10 minutes before cutting into slices to serve.

PUMPKIN SCONES

Makes 12

These scones are lovely just served with butter. I particularly like them with lemon curd and topped with a little whipped cream. Should you wish to make lemon curd, see the recipe on the following page.

30g butter
¼ cup icing sugar
1 egg, lightly whisked
2 teaspoons lemon juice
¾ cup cooked mashed pumpkin
2 cups self-raising flour
2 tablespoons milk for glazing

Heat the oven to 180°C. Grease an 18cm x 28cm lamington tray or line with baking paper.

In a bowl cream the butter and icing sugar. Add the egg, lemon juice, pumpkin and flour, mixing well to make a soft dough.

Turn out onto a lightly floured surface, sprinkle with flour and knead briefly. Pat out to 1.5cm thick. Cut 12 rounds with a scone cutter or upturned small glass regularly dipped in flour. Place on the prepared tray and brush with milk.

Bake for 15–20 minutes.

Lemon Curd
Makes about 700ml

1 teaspoon cornflour
juice of 2 lemons
2 eggs, lightly whisked
¾ cup sugar
125g butter, chopped

In a bowl dissolve the cornflour in the lemon juice, then add the rest of the ingredients.

Place all the ingredients in a small saucepan. Stir with a whisk over a low heat without allowing it to boil until the mixture thickens.

Remove from the heat and pour into sterilised jars and seal. Keep in the fridge and use within 2 weeks.

PUMPKIN, PRUNE AND WHITE CHOCOLATE SLICE

Serves 6–8

125g butter
½ cup sugar
2 eggs
½ cup cooked mashed pumpkin
2 cups self-raising flour
1 cup chopped prunes, tightly packed
¾ cup small white choc dots or chopped white chocolate
½ teaspoon vanilla extract or essence

Heat the oven to 160°C. Grease an 18cm x 28cm x 2.5cm slab tin, line the base with baking paper and grease again.

In a bowl cream the butter and sugar, then whisk in the eggs until well combined. Stir in the pumpkin, then fold in the flour, prunes, white chocolate and vanilla. Spoon into the prepared tin and smooth out. Bake for 30–40 minutes, or until a skewer inserted into the centre comes out clean.

Allow the slice to stand in the tin for 10 minutes, then turn out onto a wire rack to cool completely.

This slice is nice served cut into squares, and even nicer cut into slices and spread with butter. It also makes a good dessert if served warm with custard.

SPICED PUMPKIN PIE

Serves 6–8

1 sheet frozen sweet shortcrust pastry, thawed*
4 eggs
1 cup cooked mashed pumpkin
½ cup brown sugar
½ teaspoon ground cinnamon
½ teaspoon ground nutmeg
½ teaspoon ground ginger
½ teaspoon ground allspice
pinch of ground cloves
2 teaspoons lemon juice
1 tablespoon plain flour
30g butter, melted
½ cup milk or cream

Heat the oven to 200°C. Grease a 23cm pie dish.

Line the pie dish with the pastry and trim the edges. Refrigerate while preparing the filling.

Place the eggs in a bowl and whisk together with the pumpkin, sugar, spices, lemon juice, butter and milk. Pour into the pastry case.

Bake for 10 minutes, then reduce the heat to 150°C and bake for 20 minutes more, or until the filling is set. Allow the pie to stand for 20 minutes before cutting it into slices to serve.

Serve with sweetened whipped cream to the side, lightly dusted with a little cinnamon.

* *If preferred, make your own pastry from the recipe on page 214.*

MISCELLANEOUS VEGETABLES

Vegetable Fritters

Makes about 6–8

These fritters are delicious served with crispy bacon and eggs with grilled tomatoes.

2 cups cooked mashed vegetables
1 small onion, grated
1 cup self-raising flour
1 egg, lightly whisked
1 tablespoon lemon juice
½ teaspoon salt
canola oil for frying

In a bowl mix together the vegetables, onion, flour, egg, lemon juice and salt. Shape into patties using wet hands.

Heat the oil in a frying pan over medium-high heat. Cook the patties for 3 minutes on one side, then turn and cook them for about 2 minutes on the other side, or until golden.

Drain on absorbent kitchen paper.

MINI FRITTATAS

Makes about 18

30g butter
1 cup cooked diced vegetables
1 small onion, grated (optional)
3 eggs, lightly beaten
1 cup milk or cream
½ cup grated tasty cheese

Heat the oven to 160°C. Grease 12–18 scoop patty tins.

Melt the butter in a small saucepan over medium heat and gently sauté the vegetables and onion for 1 minute. Cool.

Add the eggs, cream, cheese and salt and pepper to taste, and combine well.

Spoon the mixture into the prepared tins and bake for about 15 minutes, or until set.

Roasted Root Vegetable Pie

Serves 4

This recipe is ideal for using up leftover roasted root vegetables. If you have any leftover gravy from the roast, this is an excellent addition to the pie filling. Also, any leftover roasted meat (cubed) can be added with the vegetables.

> 1 tablespoon olive oil
> 600g diced lean beef
> 1 onion, diced
> 2 tomatoes, diced (optional)
> 1¾ cups beef or chicken stock, water or half stock/half gravy
> **400g leftover roasted root vegetables, including pumpkin**
> **if you have it**
> 3 teaspoons cornflour mixed to a paste with 2 tablespoons of
>   cold water.
> 1 sheet frozen puff pastry, thawed

Heat the oil in a saucepan over high heat and sauté the beef until browned. Add the onion and sauté for 2 minutes more. Add the tomato and stock, and bring to the boil. Reduce the heat and simmer for 1½ hours, or until meat is tender. Stir in the leftover vegetables and bring back to the boil. If it needs thickening, stir in some or all of the cornflour paste. Add salt and pepper to taste.

Heat the oven to 200°C. Grease a 20cm casserole dish.

Pour the mixture into the prepared dish, cover with the pastry and fold in the edges to fit. With a fork prick the pastry in several places.

Bake for 20–30 minutes, or until the pastry is puffed and golden.

Roasted Vegetable and Feta Tart

Serves 6

1 sheet frozen shortcrust pastry, thawed*
1 cup diced roasted vegetables
1 medium onion, grated
1 tablespoon chopped fresh basil or parsley
½ red capsicum, diced
½ cup corn kernels
125g feta, diced
½ cup cream
¾ cup milk
4 eggs
½ teaspoon salt
2 teaspoons mayonnaise
½ cup grated tasty cheese
2 tomatoes, sliced

Heat the oven to 200°C. Grease a 23cm pie dish.

Line the pie dish with the pastry and trim the edges. Place the roasted vegetables, onion, basil, capsicum, corn and feta in a bowl and carefully mix together. Sprinkle over the base of the pastry case.

Whisk together the cream, milk, eggs, salt and mayonnaise and pour over the vegetables. Sprinkle with grated cheese and decorate with sliced tomatoes. Sprinkle with salt and pepper and a little sugar.

Bake for 10 minutes, then reduce the heat to 150°C and bake for 20 minutes more, or until the filling is set.

Serve with a green salad.

* *If preferred, make your own pastry from the recipe on page 142.*

CREAM OF VEGETABLE SOUP

Serves 4

3–4 cups cooked vegetables, mashed or diced
1 onion, grated
4 cups chicken stock, or water with 3 teaspoons stock
    powder
½ cup grated tasty cheese
½ cup cream (optional)

Place the vegetables, onion and stock in a large saucepan. Bring to the boil and cook for 5 minutes. Remove from the heat and purée.

Return the soup to the heat and bring back to the boil. Remove from heat and stir in the cheese until melted, then stir in the cream. Reheat but do not boil. Add salt and pepper to taste.

Add a little milk or extra cream if you prefer a thinner soup.

Serve sprinkled with chopped parsley or snipped chives

SALADS

Leftover salads are one of the things most frequently thrown in the bin. Green salads especially soon wilt and look most unappetising, so remember to refrigerate them as soon as possible after serving to keep them fresh.

Many years ago I had a recipe that was called Beggar's Soup, which was basically just lettuce leaves shredded and cooked in chicken stock with sliced spring onions and parsley. So next time you have a classic green salad left over, rinse off the dressing, chop it up and cook it this way to make a tasty, economical soup.

Leftover rice salad is excellent in the Spinach, Chorizo and Semi-Dried Tomato Rice Bake (page 61), instead of the plain rice.

COLESLAW TOSS

Serves 4

    3½ cups (about 500g) coleslaw
    1 tablespoon olive oil
    1 onion, diced
    125g bacon, diced

To remove any dressing, rinse the coleslaw in a sieve or colander and leave it to drain well.

Heat the oil in a frying pan over medium-high heat and sauté the onion and bacon until the onion is soft and the bacon begins to crisp. Add the drained coleslaw and cook for 5–10 minutes, or until the cabbage has softened and the liquid has evaporated.

Add salt and pepper to taste.

PASTA SALAD BAKE

Serves 4

1 tablespoon olive oil
1 onion, finely diced
125g bacon, diced
2 cups pasta salad
½ cup cream
½ cup milk
1½ tablespoons finely chopped parsley
2 tomatoes, deseeded and diced
½ teaspoon Dijon mustard
1 tablespoon tomato sauce (ketchup) or chutney
1 tablespoon lemon juice
½ cup grated parmesan cheese
½ cup grated tasty cheese

Heat the oven to 180°C. Grease a 20cm casserole or pie dish.

Heat the oil in a frying pan over medium heat and sauté the onion and bacon for 3 minutes. Remove from the heat and fold in the rest of the ingredients, except for the tasty cheese, mixing until well combined.

Pour into the prepared casserole dish and sprinkle over the tasty cheese. Bake for 25–30 minutes, or until heated through and the cheese is golden brown.

Serve with fresh salad and crusty bread rolls.

TOMATO PASTE & PASTA SAUCE

Tomato paste can add an extra subtle richness to casserole- and mince-style dishes. To make a tasty pan gravy for a roast, add 2 teaspoons tomato paste for every one and a half cups of liquid.

If you make your own pasta dough, small amounts can be incorporated to give colour and flavour.

Pasta sauce has a variety of uses. Try using it as a pie filling, with a little grated parmesan or tasty cheese sprinkled on top, then close it with a top layer of pastry, or leave it as an open pie.

Try using a Bolognese- or Napolitana-style pasta sauce as the topping for a pizza base. Even a cream style pasta sauce can be used in this way and is ideal for seafood pizzas.

Likewise, spread halved bread rolls with a pasta sauce, then add toppings and grated cheese and bake for 12–15 minutes at 190°C until heated through and cheese is bubbling and golden.

Add tomato-style pasta sauces to casserole style dishes to give extra flavour and definition to their gravies.

TOMATO PASTE

(See also Vegetarian Lasagne page 155.)

Perhaps more than any other scrapings from the jar that have been known to go to waste in our house is tomato paste. I will use part of the jar or small tin, then sometimes faithfully cover it with olive oil to preserve it longer, or if from a tin, transfer it to another container and refrigerate for later use. All too often it ends up in the bin as I've left it for too long before finding a recipe in which to use it.

Of course it can be frozen in ice cube trays, but as the amount is often minimal, I end up with only a couple of cubes filled, and then it dries out in the freezer before I get back to it.

Hence I have put together the following recipes to inspire me to use up the scrapings quickly. The tomato paste provides a subtle yet integral part of these particularly delicious dishes. The amount need not be exact — it doesn't matter if a little more or less is used.

Beef and Mushroom Pie

Pastry
90g plain flour
90g self-raising flour
½ teaspoon salt
90g butter
1 egg yolk
2 teaspoons lemon juice
¼ cup (approximately) cold water

Filling
1 tablespoon olive oil
600g diced stewing beef (such as blade, gravy beef or chuck)
1 small onion, diced
600g mushrooms, cut into 1cm dice
1 tablespoon tomato paste
2¼ cups chicken or beef stock
½ teaspoon salt
2 teaspoons cornflour

To make the pastry, mix the flours and salt together in a bowl then rub in the butter with your fingertips until the mixture resembles breadcrumbs. (If you wish, you can use a food processor up to this stage and then transfer the mixture to a bowl.) Make a well in the centre.

Whisk the egg yolk, lemon juice and half the water together in a small bowl and pour into the well in the flour. Mix through with a metal spoon or knife, adding more water only if necessary to bring the mixture together. Wrap in cling wrap and place in the fridge for at least 30 minutes.

To make the filling, heat the oil in a saucepan over medium-high heat and sauté the meat until well coloured. Add the onion and mushrooms and cook for 5 minutes more. Add the tomato paste, 2 cups of the stock and salt. Bring to the boil and simmer for approximately 2 hours, or until the meat is tender, adding a little extra stock or water if the mixture looks like it is starting to reduce too much. Mix the cornflour to a paste with the remaining (cold) stock and mix some or all of it into the beef and mushroom mixture to thicken. Add salt and pepper to taste. Cool.

To assemble the pie

Heat the oven to 200°C. Grease a 20cm pie dish.

On a lightly floured board, roll out two thirds of the pastry to line the base and sides of the pie dish. Dampen the edges with a little water or egg white. Fill with the beef and mushroom mixture. Roll out the rest of the pastry and place over the filling. Press edges together well to seal and trim excess pastry*. Prick in several places with a fork.

Bake for 10 minutes, then reduce heat to 170°C and bake for a further 20 minutes, or until the pastry is lightly browned and crisp.

Serve with creamy mashed potato and seasonal vegetables.

* *Wrap trimmings of pastry in cling wrap for later use (page 233) — it will keep well in the fridge for 2–3 days, or it can be frozen for up to 2 months.*

CALZONE WITH MUSHROOMS

Serves 4

Calzone is ideal for using up tomato paste and leftover pizza toppings.

2 cups plain flour
2 teaspoons dried yeast
1 teaspoon salt
1½ teaspoons sugar
1 tablespoon olive oil
1 cup warm water
2 teaspoons olive oil, extra
2 teaspoon butter
200g mushrooms, sliced
1 rounded tablespoon tomato paste

In a large bowl, mix together the flour, yeast, salt and sugar. Make a well in the centre and pour in the oil, together with enough of the warm water to make a soft dough. Mix well and cover the bowl with a tea towel. Leave to rise for 30–40 minutes, so it is approximately doubled in size.

Meanwhile, heat the oil and butter over medium-high heat and sauté the mushrooms for 5 minutes. Cool completely.

Heat the oven to 200°C. Oil a 25cm pizza tray.

Turn the dough out onto a lightly floured board, sprinkle with flour and knead for 2–3 minutes, or until smooth. Place on prepared tray. Pat the dough out to approximately 1cm thick. Spread with the tomato paste, leaving a 1cm margin around the edge. Spread with the mushrooms. Dampen the edge of one half of the dough and fold over the other half to enclose the filling. Press the edges together. Cover loosely with a tea towel and allow the dough to rise for 20 minutes. Bake for 20 minutes, or until it is lightly browned.

Serve with Chicken with Mushrooms and Tomatoes (page 200).

CHICKEN WITH MUSHROOMS AND TOMATOES

Serves 2 with rice or 4 with calzone

This dish is delicious served over boiled rice or pasta, but is truly exceptional served with slices of calzone (see previous page).

1 tablespoon olive oil
2 skinless chicken breasts, sliced
1 onion, diced
1 red capsicum, diced
200g mushrooms, sliced
4 medium tomatoes, diced
1 rounded tablespoon tomato paste
1½ cups chicken stock or water
3 teaspoons sweet chilli sauce
3 teaspoons Worcestershire sauce
2 teaspoons soy sauce
2 teaspoons chutney (any sort)
1 cup baby spinach leaves or 3 shredded silver beet leaves

Heat the oil over medium-high heat and sauté the chicken for 3 minutes. Add the onion, capsicum, mushrooms and tomatoes and sauté for 5 minutes more. Add the tomato paste, stock, sauces and chutney. Bring to the boil and simmer for 5 minutes. Add the baby spinach and simmer for 5 minutes more, or until the chicken is cooked.

CREAMY TOMATO SOUP

Serves 4

1 tablespoon olive oil
2 teaspoons butter
1 onion, finely diced
2 cloves garlic, crushed
2 x 410g tins diced tomatoes
2 sprigs rosemary
2 teaspoons Worcestershire sauce
2 teaspoons tomato sauce (ketchup)
3–4 teaspoons tomato paste
¾ teaspoon salt
½ teaspoon brown sugar
¼ teaspoon paprika
pinch of mustard powder
1 teaspoon sweet chilli sauce
1 cup chicken stock
½ cup pouring or thickened cream

Heat the oil and butter in a saucepan, add the onion and sauté over low heat until soft. Add the garlic and sauté for 1 minute more. Stir in the tomatoes, rosemary, sauces, tomato paste, salt, sugar, paprika, mustard, chilli sauce and chicken stock and bring to the boil. Simmer for 15 minutes. Remove the rosemary sprigs and stir in the cream. Heat again but do not allow it to boil.

Serve with fresh crusty bread. It is especially nice with Chicken with Mushrooms and Tomatoes (see previous page).

MINESTRONE

Serves 4

2 tablespoons olive oil
1 chorizo sausage, diced (optional)
1 onion, finely diced
4 tablespoons chopped bacon
1 carrot, diced
1 small potato, diced
1 red capsicum, diced
125g green beans, sliced
4 cloves garlic, crushed
1 rounded tablespoon tomato paste
½ teaspoon dried thyme or 2 teaspoons chopped fresh thyme
½ teaspoon sugar
410g tin crushed or diced tomatoes
3 cups chicken stock, or water mixed with 2 teaspoons stock
    powder
2 cups cooked pasta (such as macaroni or spiralli)
½ cup shaved parmesan cheese
2 tablespoons chopped parsley to serve (optional)

Heat the oil in a large saucepan over medium-high heat and sauté the chorizo, if using, onion and bacon for 5 minutes. Add the vegetables and continue to cook gently for 5 minutes. Add the garlic and sauté for 1 minute more. Stir in the tomato paste, thyme, sugar, tomatoes and stock. Bring to the boil and simmer for 10 minutes. Stir in the pasta, bring back to the boil and simmer for 3 minutes more. Add salt and pepper to taste.

Serve in individual bowls, sprinkled with parmesan and chopped parsley. Fresh crusty bread is an ideal accompaniment.

Mini Pizzas

Makes about 18

2 sheets frozen puff pastry, thawed
2 tablespoons tomato paste
3 tablespoons tomato purée
¼ teaspoon salt
pinch of sugar
½ teaspoon chopped fresh rosemary or 1 teaspoon chopped
    fresh basil
a little grated mozzarella or tasty cheese to taste

Toppings
chopped salami
finely diced onion
finely diced ham or bacon
finely diced pineapple
finely diced deseeded tomato
anchovy strips
diced cooked chicken
small pieces of seafood

Heat the oven to 200°C. Line 2 baking trays with baking paper.

With a scone cutter, cut 9 circles from each sheet of pastry and place on the prepared baking trays.

In a bowl mix together the tomato paste, tomato purée, salt, sugar and herbs.

Spread the pastry rounds with a little of the tomato mixture. Top with a little cheese, then sprinkle with the toppings of your choice. It is best to put the meat toppings on before the vegetable ones. Top with grated cheese. Seafood should be added last and not covered with cheese.

Bake for about 12 minutes, or until they are puffed and the cheese is melted.

Hint *Do not overload with toppings as this will cause the bases to be soggy.*

QUICK BOLOGNESE SAUCE

Serves 4

1 tablespoon olive oil
250g best minced beef
250g minced pork
100g bacon, diced
1 onion, finely diced
2 large cloves garlic, crushed
400g tin diced tomatoes
1 tablespoon tomato paste
½ cup beef stock or water
2 teaspoons chutney (any sort)
2 teaspoons Worcestershire sauce
1 teaspoon dried oregano

Heat the oil in a saucepan over medium-high heat and sauté the minces with the bacon and onion until the mince changes colour. Add the garlic and sauté for 1 minute more. Add the tomatoes, tomato paste, stock, chutney, sauce and oregano.

Bring to the boil and simmer uncovered for 30 minutes.

Serve with fettuccini or spaghetti and top each serve with freshly grated parmesan cheese.

PASTA SAUCE

PASTICCIO

Serves 4

2 cups (appromimately) leftover Bolognese sauce
125g (approximately) instant lasagne sheets
1½ cups milk
3 teaspoons cornflour mixed to a paste with 2 tablespoons of
    cold milk
1 cup grated tasty cheese

Heat the oven to 170°C. Grease a 20cm square baking dish.

Place ½ cup of the Bolognese sauce in the base of the dish. Cover with one layer of lasagne sheets, then spread over the remaining Bolognese sauce. Cover with another layer of lasagne sheets.

Heat the milk in a medium saucepan to boiling point, and while boiling whisk in the cornflour paste until the sauce thickens. Stir in half of the cheese and keep stirring until melted. Add salt and white pepper to taste. Spread over the lasagne sheets and sprinkle with the remaining cheese.

Bake for 30 minutes, or until the lasagne sheets are cooked. Allow to stand for 10 minutes before cutting into squares to serve.

Serve with salad and garlic bread.

Sloppy Joes

Serves 4

Sloppy Joes were invented and named by our children when they were young. It is not only a good way to use up Bolognese sauce, but also bread rolls that are going a little stale.

Although this recipe specifies using Bolognese sauce, other types of pasta sauce can be substituted. The sauce can also be topped with other ingredients, such as salami, capsicum, olives and so on.

> 4 large bread rolls, such as hamburger buns
> **1½ cups (approximately) Bolognese or Napolitana sauce**
> ¾ cup grated tasty or mozzarella cheese

Heat the oven to 170°C. Line 2 baking trays with baking paper.

Cut the rolls in half and spread with the Bolognese sauce. Sprinkle with the grated cheese and bake for 12–15 minutes, or until heated through and the cheese is melted.

TACO NACHO SAUCE

Makes 2 cups

The addition of various herbs and spices to a Bolognese sauce turns it into a Mexican-style sauce, ideal for topping tacos or nachos. It is also a very good topping for potatoes cooked in their jackets.

    1 tablespoon olive oil
    2 teaspoons ground cumin
    1 teaspoon ground oregano
    ½ teaspoon ground coriander
    1 tablespoon sweet chilli sauce
    1½ cups Bolognese sauce
    ½ cup water

Heat the oil in a saucepan over medium heat and sauté the spices for 1 minute. Add the chilli sauce, Bolognese sauce and water, and bring to the boil. Simmer for 3 minutes. Add salt and pepper to taste.

TORTILLA BAKE

Serves 4

This tasty dish makes a little Bolognese sauce go a long, long way.

125g plain flour
¼ teaspoon salt
2 eggs
1 cup water
1½–2 cups Bolognese sauce
½ cup finely diced ham or salami
400g tin tomatoes
1 tablespoon tomato paste
1 onion, grated
2 teaspoons chutney (any sort)
½ cup grated tasty cheese
⅓ cup grated parmesan cheese

Place the flour, salt, eggs and water in a mixing bowl and beat until smooth. Transfer the mixture to a jug.

Spray a large frying pan with cooking oil (or use a non-stick pan) and heat over medium-high heat. Pour approximately 2 tablespoons of pancake batter into the pan and tilt the pan to spread out to a large round. Cook on one side for 3 minutes, then turn and cook for 1 minute on the other side. Repeat until all the mixture is used. Set aside and keep warm.

Heat the oven to 170°C. Grease a 20cm square lasagne dish.

Mix together the Bolognese sauce and ham. Spread over the entire surface of each pancake and roll up. Place side by side in the dish. Mix together the tomatoes, tomato paste, onion, chutney and salt and pepper to taste and spoon over the tortillas. Sprinkle with the combined cheeses and bake for 30 minutes, or until the cheese is golden.

Serve with a green salad and garlic bread.

SWEET LEFTOVERS & PASTRY

Leftover cake can often be warmed and served with custard or ice cream to make a dessert.

There is no need to throw away stale biscuits – restore them to their fresh, baked condition by simply placing several of them on a microwave safe tray and heating them on High for 1–2 minutes, depending on the quantity. If however, you only have a few left in the jar, try using them in the super delicious Cranachan (page 213).

Scones can be reheated in the microwave for a few seconds per scone, or brushed with milk and reheated in a slow oven for a few minutes. Use cooked plain scones as a topping for a casserole-type dish. Place on top of the savoury mixture, then brush their tops with milk and bake for 20 minutes at 160°C. Similarly, sweet or fruit (or even pumpkin) scones can be used as part of a fruit 'cobbler'. Simply place about 2 cupfuls of any sort of stewed fruit, sweetened to taste, in a casserole or pie dish and top with the scones. Brush the tops with milk, sprinkle with a little sugar and cinnamon if desired, and bake at 160°C for 20 minutes.

To use up small pieces of frozen puff pastry sheets, don't scrunch them together but rather stack up the bits and pieces, dusting the top and base of the pile with just a little flour and re-roll. The same applies to shortcrust pastry. Sweet shortcrust pastry scraps can be re-rolled to make kiss biscuits or little sweet tart cases (page 234).

CAKES, BISCUITS AND SCONES

It can certainly be tempting to just throw out leftover bits and pieces of cakes and biscuits. However, biscuits generally keep well in an airtight container or you can freeze them until you are ready to use them up, and leftover scones are very versatile. I always freeze leftover pieces of cake for later use in rum balls. They are very quick to make, and have the added advantage of needing no baking.

STROGANOFF WITH SCONE TOPPING

Serves 4–6

2 tablespoons olive oil
1kg lean blade steak (or similar), diced
2 onions, diced
2 cloves garlic, crushed
350g mushrooms, sliced
3 tablespoons tomato paste
2 cups beef or chicken stock or water
1 teaspoon salt
3 teaspoons Worcestershire sauce
2 teaspoons chutney
4–6 scones
3 teaspoons cornflour mixed to a paste with about
    2 tablespoons of cold water
4 tablespoons sour cream

In a saucepan heat the oil over medium-high heat and sauté the meat until it browns, add the onion, garlic and mushrooms and sauté for 2 minutes more.

Mix in the tomato paste, stock or water, salt, Worcestershire sauce and chutney, and simmer, covered, for 1½–2 hours, or until the meat is tender.

Brush the tops of the scones with a little milk or water and place on top of the stroganoff. Replace the lid and simmer for 5 minutes more. Remove the scones with a slotted spoon and keep warm.

Thicken the stroganoff if required by stirring in some or all of the cornflour paste, then stir in the sour cream. Add salt and pepper to taste. Top each serve of stroganoff with a scone.

Serve with seasonal vegetables.

BISCUIT CRUMB CRUST FOR CHEESECAKE

Serves 6

This crumb crust is a quick base for a cold pie filling or cheesecake.

250g plain sweet biscuit crumbs
100g melted butter

Combine well and press into a 20cm pie dish or base of a 20–23cm cake tin. Refrigerate until firm.

For a simple cheesecake filling
395g tin condensed milk
½ cup lemon juice
250g cream cheese, softened
4 teaspoons gelatine powder
½ cup boiling water

In a bowl whisk together the condensed milk, lemon juice and cream cheese until very smooth.

In a small bowl sprinkle the gelatine over the boiling water and whisk until the gelatine dissolves. Add to the cream cheese mixture and stir until it is well combined.

Pour into the chilled crust and refrigerate until set. Top with fresh seasonal fruits.

CRANACHAN

Serves 4

Cranachan is a famous Scottish dessert, traditionally served at New Year. Instead of the toasted oats that are the usual ingredient, I have used leftover and crumbed Anzac biscuits or similar biscuits for a nutty caramel turn of flavour. The whisky can be left out if being served to children.

> 250g raspberries, fresh is best, but frozen will do
> 1 cup thickened cream
> 2 tablespoons honey
> 2 tablespoons whisky (optional)
> **4 (approximately) Anzac or similar biscuits**

In the base of each of 4 parfait glasses, place 2 teaspoons of raspberries.

Place the cream in a bowl and whisk until firm peaks form. Add the honey and whisky and fold in until the mixture becomes soft and creamy. Fold in the rest of the raspberries and half the biscuit crumbs to make a rippled effect.

Spoon into the parfait glasses, smooth over the top and sprinkle over the remaining crumbs. Refrigerate for at least 3 hours before serving.

Serve topped with extra berries if desired.

FRANGIPANE TART WITH SEASONAL FRUITS

Serves 6

For the pastry*
60g butter
60g sugar
1 egg yolk
125g plain flour
1 teaspoon baking powder

For the filling and topping
125g butter
100g icing sugar
1 egg
1 egg yolk
60g almond meal
1½ cups cake crumbs
1½ cups sweetened whipped cream
fresh seasonal fruit (optional)

To make the pastry, cream the butter and sugar, then whisk in the egg yolk. Combine the flour and baking powder and fold into the creamed mixture. Wrap in cling wrap and place in the fridge for 30 minutes.

Heat the oven to 190°C. Grease a 23cm pie dish.

On a lightly floured surface, roll out the pastry to fit the base and sides of the pie dish. Trim excess. (This excess can be wrapped in cling wrap and placed in the fridge for later, but use within 3 days.)

To make the filling, cream the butter and icing sugar together in a large bowl, then whisk in the egg and egg yolk. Fold in the almond meal and cake crumbs until well combined. Pour into the pastry shell.

Bake for 10 minutes, then reduce heat to 150°C and bake for 20 minutes more, or until the filling is set. Cool completely.

Spread the cream over the tart. If using, slice the fruit and place decoratively over the top of the tart.

* *Or use a sheet of thawed frozen shortcrust pastry, instead of making your own.*

Hazelnut and Sultana Dream Slices

Makes 16–20 squares

1 tablespoon honey
90g butter
100g chocolate, broken into small pieces
180g biscuit crumbs
1 cup sultanas
¼ cup desiccated coconut
½ cup roughly chopped hazelnuts

Grease an 18cm square tin and line with baking paper, then grease again.

In a saucepan melt the honey, butter and chocolate together over low heat while constantly stirring. Add the biscuit crumbs, sultanas, coconut and hazelnuts and mix until combined. Spoon the mixture evenly into the prepared tin and smooth the surface.

If the weather is warm, refrigerate until it is set. Cut into small squares to serve.

Store in an airtight container for up to 7 days.

ROCKY ROAD FUDGE

Makes about 20 squares

125g marshmallows
125g dark chocolate
200ml condensed milk
1 cup biscuit crumbs
⅓ cup slivered almonds
⅓ cup chopped glace cherries
¼ cup desiccated coconut

Grease a 20cm square tin, line with baking paper, and grease again.

Cut each marshmallow into 4 pieces.*

Break up the chocolate and place in a bowl over a saucepan of simmering water to melt. Do not allow base of the bowl to touch the water.

Remove from heat and cool slightly, then mix in the condensed milk, biscuit crumbs, almonds, cherries and coconut. Fold in the marshmallows.

Spoon the mixture into the prepared tin and spread out evenly. Allow it to set then cut into small squares to serve.

Store in an airtight container for up to 7 days.

* *To prevent the scissors sticking to the marshmallow, dip the blades occasionally into boiling water.*

WINE TRIFLE

Serves 6

250g (approximately) cake
2 tablespoons sherry
¼ cup raspberry jam
8 tinned or bottled apricot halves or sliced peaches, drained
1 packet strawberry or raspberry jelly crystals (preferably with
    no artificial colours, flavours or preservatives)
1½ cups boiling water
2¼ cups milk
2 tablespoons custard powder
¼ cup sugar
1½ cups cream
2 teaspoons icing sugar
30g dark chocolate, grated, or fresh seasonal fruits, sliced or
    diced

Cut the cake into 1cm thick slices and spread with the jam. Cut the slices
into 2cm squares and place in the base of a glass serving bowl jam side up.
Sprinkle with the sherry and arrange the apricot halves or peach slices over
the top.

Make the jelly up with the boiling water, stirring until the crystals dissolve.
Place in the fridge to cool and half set, then pour over the mixture in the
serving bowl. Place in the fridge to set completely.

Meanwhile, make the custard by bringing 2 cups of the milk to the boil in a
saucepan.

In a small bowl mix the custard powder with the remaining ¼ cup of milk to
form a thin paste. Whisk the paste into the boiling milk and keep whisking
until the custard thickens. Add the sugar and stir until dissolved, adding

extra sugar if desired. Remove from the heat. Cover the surface of the custard with cling wrap and leave it to cool completely.

Remove the set jelly mixture from the fridge and pour the cold custard over it. Cover the surface with cling wrap and return the trifle to the fridge for 30 minutes or more.

In a bowl whisk the cream with the icing sugar until it forms soft peaks. Spread over the custard. Sprinkle with the grated chocolate or decorate with fresh fruit.

Place in the fridge until ready to serve.

RUM BALLS

Makes about 24

100g dark chocolate
200g cake crumbs
2 teaspoons seedless jam
1½ tablespoons rum
1 cup (approximately) desiccated coconut

Break up the chocolate and place in a bowl over a saucepan of simmering water to melt. Do not allow the base of the bowl to touch the water.

Remove the bowl from the saucepan and add the cake crumbs, jam and rum and mix well.

Allow the mixture to stand until it is firm enough to handle, then shape into walnut-sized balls and roll in the coconut.

Store in an airtight container in the fridge for up to 2 weeks.

PAVLOVA

KNICKERBOCKER GLORY

Whenever I cook pavlova, I invariably have some left over. This recipe is a good way to use it up and it looks spectacular when layered with the other ingredients in parfait or dessert glasses. If you don't have enough pavlova for the number of people you are serving, top up with strawberry ice cream or jelly.

pavlova (with or without cream and fruit)
raspberries, fresh or frozen
vanilla ice cream (or any fruit ice cream)
cream, whipped and sweetened to taste
chocolate shavings or passionfruit pulp (optional)

Prepare parfait or dessert glasses. Layer the ingredients in a glass as follows:
Raspberries
Pavlova
Raspberries
Pavlova
Raspberries
Ice cream or sweetened whipped cream
Raspberries
Chocolate shavings

VARIATION

Layers of chopped, set jelly can be included as another layer – red or green is ideal.

CHOCOLATE

Save up scraps of chocolate to make these recipes.

CHOCOLATE GANACHE

This rich chocolate sauce can be used warm as a sauce for pouring over ice cream or a chocolate cake. If left to cool, it can be whipped to make a sensational icing for a cake. If allowed to get completely cold, it sets like fudge. You can also add a little liqueur for extra depth of flavour.

> **chocolate pieces**
> equal weight in cream

Chop the chocolate into small chunks.

Heat the cream in a saucepan until it boils. Remove from the heat and mix in the chocolate, stirring until it is melted.

Use straightaway or store in the fridge for up to 7 days.

Hint: *To re-melt the ganache, microwave on High in 20 second bursts until the desired consistency is reached.*

Chocolate Fondant Puddings

Serves 4

Success with these puddings escaped me for many years, but finally for the purposes of using up scraps of chocolate or choc dots, I managed to succeed with the following recipe. It is essential to chill the puddings for at least an hour before baking – this keeps the centre cold enough not to overcook, so that it achieves the oozy filling that makes this pudding a delight to eat.*

I have tried freezing the puddings before cooking them, but that didn't work so well.

For this recipe I use four 180ml-capacity metal dariole moulds.

> **60g chocolate scraps**
> 60g butter
> 2 eggs
> 60g caster sugar
> 10g cocoa powder
> 50g plain flour
> 2 teaspoons boiling water

Cut out 4 circles of baking paper to fit the bases of 4 x 180ml dariole moulds or ramekins. Grease each mould well, place a paper circle in each base, and grease again.

Place the chocolate and butter in a medium bowl over a saucepan of simmering water but do not let the water touch the base of the bowl. Stir occasionally until the chocolate is melted. Remove from the heat and cool but do not allow it to set.

In a bowl beat the eggs and sugar together until thick and creamy, then fold into the chocolate and butter mixture. Sift the cocoa and flour together and fold into the mixture until well combined. Drizzle the boiling water down the inside of the bowl and mix through gently.

Divide the mixture between the dariole moulds. Cover with cling wrap and refrigerate for at least 1 hour.

Heat the oven to 180°C.

Remove the cling wrap and bake for 9 minutes. Remove from the oven, leave in the moulds for 2 minutes, then invert onto serving plates. Serve with vanilla ice cream or mascarpone.

*Hint: *Just in case the puddings do not have the oozy middle, all is not lost. Serve them as chocolate puddings, drizzled with ganache (page 220), ice cream and fresh berries or other seasonal fruits. There will be no complaints to be sure.*

Jaffa Pudding with Chocolate Sauce

Serves 6—8

125g butter
1½ cups sugar
¼ cup cocoa powder
½ teaspoon bicarbonate of soda
60g chocolate scraps
¾ cup water
¼ cup orange juice
2 teaspoons finely grated orange rind
2 eggs, lightly beaten
2 cups self-raising flour

Heat the oven to 180°C. Grease a deep 20cm cake tin and line the base with baking paper, then grease again.

Place the butter, sugar, cocoa, bicarbonate of soda, chocolate, water and orange juice in a large saucepan. Bring to the boil, stirring. Turn the heat down and simmer for 2 minutes, then turn off the heat and leave to stand for 10 minutes.

Add the orange rind, eggs and self-raising flour and whisk until smooth.

Pour into the prepared tin and bake for 30 minutes, or until a metal skewer inserted into the centre comes out clean. Leave to stand in the tin for 10 minutes, then invert onto a serving plate.

Sauce
125ml cream
2 teaspoons grated orange rind
125g chocolate pieces, chopped
1–2 tablespoons Grand Marnier, brandy or orange juice

In a small saucepan, heat the cream and orange rind to boiling point. Remove from heat and strain out the orange rind, then return the cream to the heat and bring back to the boil.

Remove from the heat and add the chocolate. Stir until the chocolate melts.

Add the Grand Marnier, brandy or orange juice and mix well.

To serve, place wedges of the cake on individual serving plates and drizzle with the sauce. Serve with sweetened whipped cream or mascarpone.

Vanilla Chocolate Fudge

Makes 8—10

You can also halve the following recipes to make a smaller amount, in which case use a smaller container in which to set the fudge.

> **300g chocolate**
> 15g butter, diced
> 1 cup condensed milk
> ½ teaspoon vanilla extract or essence

Line a 15cm square tin with baking paper.

Place the chocolate in a bowl over a saucepan of simmering water but do not let the water touch the base of the bowl. When melted, remove from the heat and mix in the butter, stirring until melted, then whisk in the condensed milk and vanilla.

Pour into the prepared tin and smooth out evenly. If the mixture tends to stick to your fingers or the spoon, place a piece of cling wrap over the top and use this to smooth the surface, then remove the cling wrap.

VARIATION

Whisky and Hazelnut Fudge

Make the fudge, omitting the vanilla and instead mixing in 60g chopped hazelnuts and 3 teaspoons of whisky.

JELLY

Often after a child's party I would have bits of jelly left over. The following recipes are ways of using up these jelly scraps.

STAINED GLASS CHEESECAKE

Serves 8

Any colour jelly can be used in this cheesecake. It looks spectacular when cut into serves.

Pastry*
60g butter
60g sugar
1 egg yolk
60g plain flour
60g self-raising flour

Filling
250g cream cheese, softened
380g tin condensed milk
juice of 3 lemons
3 teaspoons gelatine
¼ cup boiling water
1½ cups firm set jelly

In a bowl cream the butter and sugar until light and fluffy, then whisk in the egg yolk. Fold in the flours and gently mix until a soft dough is formed. Wrap the dough in cling wrap and place in the fridge for 30 minutes at least.

Heat the oven to 160°C. Grease a 20cm round springform cake tin.

Roll the pastry to 4mm thickness on a lightly floured board to line the base of the prepared cake tin. Place in the tin, trim excess, prick several times with a fork, and bake for 10 minutes or until just cooked through.

Remove from the oven and cool.

In a bowl combine the cream cheese, condensed milk and lemon juice, and whisk until smooth.

Sprinkle the gelatine over the water and whisk to dissolve. Whisk into the cream cheese mixture.

Allow to stand for 5 minutes, then pour over the cooked and cooled biscuit base.

Turn the jelly out onto a plate and cut into 1cm cubes. Carefully fold through the cheesecake.

Place in the fridge for several hours to set.

* *You can use a thawed sheet of frozen shortcrust pastry instead of making your own or use the Biscuit Crumb Crust recipe on page 212.*

BUTTERFLY CAKES

Makes about 24

1 egg
¾ cup sugar
1½ cups self-raising flour
¾ cup milk
60g butter, melted
1 cup cream
1 teaspoon icing sugar
extra icing sugar for dusting
2 tablespoons (approximately) set red or green jelly

Heat the oven to 180°C. Line 24 x ¼-cup capacity patty tins with party cake papers.

Briefly whisk together the egg and sugar in a bowl, then add the flour, milk and butter and whisk until smooth.

Fill each paper case two thirds full with the cake mixture.

Bake for 12 minutes or until a metal skewer inserted into the centre comes out clean.

Remove from the oven and cool on a wire rack.

To make the filling, whisk the cream with icing sugar in a bowl until firm peaks form.

When the cakes are cold, cut a disk out of the top of each. Cut each of these in half to make two triangles or 'butterfly wings'.

Fill the hole in the cake with a little cream, and position the two 'wings' coming out of the cream, leaving a small space between them. Dust with sieved icing sugar.

Place ½ teaspoon jelly in the centre of each cake, and serve.

PASTRY

Puff pastry

———————————— ◆ ————————————

MATCHSTICKS

It seems that I often end up with just 1 sheet of puff pastry in a packet frozen in the freezer. If I leave it there, it will without fail dry out to the point of being unusable, no matter how well I have rewrapped it. Therefore, before this happens I make matchsticks from it. They will keep for up to 2 weeks if stored in an airtight container, at the ready to make a quick dessert or afternoon tea treat.

1 sheet frozen puff pastry, thawed

Heat the oven to 200°C.

Thaw the pastry sheet on a board.

Cut each pastry sheet as follows:

1	2
3	4
5	6
7	8
9	10

Bake for about 10 minutes, until the matchsticks are puffed and golden. Allow to cool completely. Store in an airtight container.

Suggestions for using
200ml cream
2 teaspoons icing sugar
3 tablespoons jam
2 teaspoons icing sugar, extra for dusting

In a bowl whip the cream with the sugar until firm peaks form.

Split the matchsticks in half and spread a little jam along the bottom half of each.

Pipe the cream over the jam and place the top half of the pastry stick on top.

Dust sieved icing sugar over the top.

CREAM HORNS

This recipe, like Matchsticks, is good for using up full or half sheets of puff pastry. To make the cream horns you will need cream horn tins, available at most supermarkets and certainly at kitchen supply stores. They usually come quite inexpensively in packs of 6. One sheet of pastry will make about 10 cream horn pastry cases.

They look sensational when filled with a little jam, sweetened whipped cream and finished with a whole or half a strawberry, then dusted with sifted icing sugar.

> **puff pastry sheet – half or whole**
> raspberry or strawberry jam
> sweetened whipped cream
> icing sugar
> small whole strawberries

Cut the pastry the full length of the sheet into 1cm strips.

Grease the outside of as many cream horn tins as you have pastry strips.

Heat the oven to 200°C. Line a baking tray with baking paper.

Wind the pastry strips around the cream horn tins and place a little apart, seam side down on the baking tray. Bake for 10–12 minutes, or until puffed and golden. Remove from the oven and take the pastry off the moulds. If they appear to be stuck, give the pastry a slight twist using a tea towel. If they are still a little moist on the inside, return the pastry case to the oven and bake for 2 minutes more or until dried out completely. Transfer to a wire rack to cool. Use immediately or store in an airtight container for up to 2 weeks.

Close to serving time, place ¼ teaspoon jam in the base, pipe cream to fill, then dust with sifted icing sugar. Place a strawberry on top of each cream horn.

Hint: *Sometimes before filling the cream horns, I dip one side in melted chocolate and leave it to set on foil or baking paper. I then fill them as usual.*

Savoury Sippets

Scraps of **puff pastry** of any shape can be baked in the oven at 200°C until they are puffed and golden. These are handy to quickly reheat and place on top of individual servings of a casserole- or stew-type dish to make an instant 'pie'. They can even be used as a topping for hot stewed fruit.

Before baking, the pastry can be also topped with grated cheese and sprinkled with paprika. These make an excellent accompaniment to soup.

Store in airtight containers. Those without cheese will keep well for 2 weeks at least.

Shortcrust pastry

♦

SAVOURY SHORTCRUST PASTRY

With a scone cutter, cut out rounds from re-rolled pastry.

Place on baking trays lined with baking paper and bake in a moderate oven until golden. Store in an airtight container. They can then be used as a base for canapés. Try for instance:

- Equal parts of cream cheese and crème fraîche or sour cream creamed together with 1 teaspoon lemon juice. Top with smoked salmon or trout and a sprig of dill.

- A small amount of horseradish cream, a slice of smoked beef and finely chopped tomato mixed with chopped fresh herbs.

- Spread with pesto and top with sliced or diced semi-dried tomatoes and top with a sliver of shaved parmesan cheese.

- Alternatively, cut rounds to line greased patty pans. These will need to be blind baked. My pastry chef son showed me a trick that revolutionised this for me: half fill the paper cases with dried beans or uncooked rice, and place a paper case in each unbaked pastry case. Bake for 10–12 minutes, or until golden brown. Amazingly logical and easy. These pastries can be stored in an airtight container for 2 weeks. For a hot savoury, fill with a savoury filling such as Bolognese Sauce (page 204) or Tuna Mornay (page 151), top with a little grated cheese and bake for 7 minutes or until bubbling.

SWEET SHORTCRUST PASTRY

Roll out scraps of leftover pastry and cut into rounds. They can then be used in any of the following ways:

To make **kiss biscuits**, bake in a moderate oven on baking trays lined with baking paper for 10 minutes, or until golden. When cool, join pairs of biscuits together with jam, ice with pink icing and sprinkle with hundreds and thousands.

To make **funny face biscuits**, bake for 10 minutes in a moderate oven and cool completely. Make some pink icing and provide a variety of lollies. Spread the biscuits with the icing and let children decorate them for themselves.

To make **pastry cases**, line ¼-cup capacity patty tins with pastry rounds. Place a paper case half filled with dried beans or uncooked rice in each unbaked pastry case. Bake for 10–12 minutes or until golden and crisp. When cool, they can be stored in an airtight container for up to 2 weeks. At serving time, fill with, for instance, jam and whipped cream or Lemon Curd (page 185).

To fill **pastry cases** as above, mix cream cheese with a little lemon juice and icing sugar to taste. Place a teaspoonful in each tart and decorate with seasonal fruits. If not to be served immediately, the tarts should be glazed with a little sieved apricot jam to stop the fruit from drying out.

Filo pastry

I always end up with a few sheets of filo pastry left over that I faithfully wrap up tightly in cling wrap and place in the fridge for later use. Almost inevitably it goes mouldy before I get to it. With the following easy recipe for a very simple Apple Strudel this need never happen again.

These are not exactly traditional strudels in that they are not rolled up to enclose the filling, but rather they have a top and bottom layer of pastry which I find much easier to handle.

Use the strudel as a dessert and any leftovers as an afternoon tea treat.

CHICKEN AND VEGETABLE STRUDEL

Serves 4–6

This recipe is also good for using up leftover cooked chicken (about 250g) and leftover vegetables (1 cup) if you have them on hand. Otherwise, use the recipe as follows.

1½ cups milk
3 teaspoons cornflour mixed to a paste with 2 tablespoons of cold milk
½ cup grated tasty cheese
1 tablespoon parmesan cheese
1 tablespoon ricotta cheese (optional)
¼ teaspoon salt
1 tablespoon olive oil
2 skinless chicken breast fillets, diced
1 cup finely diced mixed raw vegetables (such as carrot, pumpkin, sweet potato, capsicum)
2 spring onions, finely slice, or 1 onion, grated
1 tablespoon lemon juice
1 tablespoon shredded fresh basil (optional)
½ cup fresh breadcrumbs
6 sheets filo pastry
1 tablespoon milk, extra
1 tablespoon sesame seeds

Heat the oven to 180°C. Line a baking tray with baking paper.

Heat the milk in a medium saucepan, and when boiling whisk in the cornflour paste until the mixture thickens. Stir in the cheeses until melted. Add the salt and white pepper to taste. Place a piece of cling wrap on the surface and allow to cool completely.

Meanwhile, heat the oil in a frying pan over medium-high heat and sauté the chicken and vegetables for 5 minutes. Mix into the cheese sauce, together with the spring onion, lemon juice, basil and breadcrumbs. Add salt and pepper to taste, and cool.

Place 1 sheet of pastry on the tray, spray with cooking oil, place another sheet on top and spray again, then top with a final sheet. Brush edges with a little water.

Spoon the chicken and vegetable filling over the pastry, leaving a 1cm strip free around the outer edge.

Place 1 sheet of filo pastry on a lightly floured surface, spray with cooking oil, place another sheet on top and spray again, then top with a final sheet. Place this pastry stack over the filling and press the edges of the top and bottom pastry together to seal. Brush with milk and sprinkle with sesame seeds.

Bake for 30 minutes, or until golden. Remove from oven and stand for 10 minutes before cutting into squares to serve.

VARIATION

Cooked seafood can be substituted for the chicken in this recipe, in which case the herb could be changed to dill instead of basil.

APPLE STRUDEL

Serves 4–6

700g apples, peeled and cored
2 teaspoons finely grated lemon rind
⅓ cup sugar
½ cup **fresh breadcrumbs**
2 teaspoons ground cinnamon
3 teaspoons lemon juice
¼ cup ground almonds
45g butter, melted
6 sheets filo pastry
½ teaspoon ground cinnamon, extra
2 teaspoons sugar, extra

Heat the oven to 180°C. Line a baking tray with baking paper.

Dice the apples, then mix in a bowl with the lemon rind, sugar, breadcrumbs, cinnamon, lemon juice, almonds and 30g of the butter.

Place 1 sheet of pastry on the tray, spray with cooking oil, place another sheet on top and spray again, then top with a final sheet. Spoon the apple filling onto this, leaving a 1cm strip free around the outer edges. Brush edges with a little water.

Place 1 sheet of pastry on a lightly floured surface, spray with cooking oil, place another sheet of pastry on top and spray again, then top with a final sheet. Place this pastry stack over the apple filling and press the edges of the top and bottom pastry together to seal, folding in edges if necessary.

Brush the top with the remaining butter. Mix together the extra cinnamon and sugar and sprinkle over the top. Bake for 30 minutes, or until golden.

Remove from the oven and stand for 10 minutes before cutting into squares to serve.

FRUIT

Fresh fruit can be used to make a fruit salad. Try freezing bits and pieces to later make into jam – it is very simple to do. Virtually any combination of fruit can be used to make an interesting array of delicious jams. To make jam, simply soften the fruit with a ¼ cup of water and the juice of a lemon over a low heat. Once softened, add the sugar. A good rule of thumb is to add an equal weight of sugar to the fruit you have used. Bring to the boil, stirring, and boil briskly until the setting point is reached. Frozen citrus fruits, even just the peels, can be used to make marmalade (see recipes on pages 246 and 260).

Fruit can also be steeped in alcohol and sugar which makes a wonderful accompaniment to a rich ice cream or whipped cream, or it can be served in small amounts with meat dishes. Simply layer fruit in a very clean jar with sugar, and cover with brandy, gin, vodka or rum. The proportions are: 500–600g of fruit, 250g of sugar and 300ml of spirit. Store in a cool dark place for 3 months before using. The amount of sugar can be reduced a little if desired.

Stewed fruits can be frozen for later use in pies and crumbles. At times it may be necessary to thicken the mixture, otherwise the pastry or crumble topping may become soggy. To do this, bring to the boil and thicken by stirring in a little cornflour mixed to a paste with cold water. Cool before using as a filling for a sweet pastry crust. For crumbles it is fine to use it hot.

Bottled, tinned and stewed fruits can be mixed into yoghurt or pureed and mixed with whipped cream to make an old fashioned fruit 'fool'.

FRESH, PART OR WHOLE FRUIT

Keeping in mind how important it is to include fruit in a healthy diet, I always enthusiastically buy up whenever I visit the market. Actually, I tend to buy a bit too much and often risk wasting it. Sometimes I've managed to stew the excess, but often there are stray pieces of single fresh fruit left in the bowl needing something done with them.

The following recipes are ones that I have put together for such times; they range from fresh fruit to stewed, to those small amounts of dried fruit left in a packet. There is really no need to waste a single piece of fruit, as it can be held in 'suspended animation' ready to be made into a delicious jam, jelly, marmalade or chutney. If you don't have enough for a whole batch, freeze the piece of fruit until you have enough to make a few jars. Even peels and cores of many fruits can be used.

BANANA, CHEESE AND BACON ON TOAST

Serves 4

Although this may sound an unusual combination, it was a real favourite with our children as a snack or light lunch.

4–5 slices stale bread
2 large ripe bananas, mashed
125g bacon, diced
1½ cups grated tasty cheese

Toast the bread on one side until golden, then turn and very lightly toast the other side.

Mix together the banana, bacon and half the cheese. Spread on the lightly toasted side of the toast and sprinkle with the remaining cheese.

Place under the griller and cook until the topping is bubbling and the cheese topping is golden brown.

FRESH FRUIT SALAD

Serves 2

½ cup sugar
½ cup water
2 teaspoons lemon juice
**2–3 cups diced fresh fruit (such as apples, pears, oranges,
mandarins, kiwi fruit, strawberries, pineapple, mango)**

In a small saucepan bring the sugar, water and lemon juice to the boil.
Simmer for 1 minute. Cool.

Place the fruits in a serving bowl, pour the cooled sugar syrup over and mix
together gently.

Serve with yoghurt, whipped cream or ice cream.

LUMBERJACK CAKE

Serves 8—10

Although this cake is traditionally made with apples, I love it made with firm fleshed pears and flavoured with lime rind. I have also made it very successfully with bananas, cut into 1cm dice (you will need about 3 bananas). I am sure it would work well with other fruits such as mango, pawpaw or pineapple or a combination of these that total about 200g. I would not use citrus fruits, however. All things considered, it is a delicious cake that can be made from, for instance, the leftovers from a fruit platter or pieces of fruit left in the fruit bowl.

The cake will keep well for several days in an airtight container in the fridge.

1 teaspoon bicarbonate of soda
¾ cup boiling water
1½ cups chopped dates
125g butter
1 cup brown sugar
2 eggs
2 apples or pears, cored and finely chopped
1½ cups self-raising flour
1 teaspoon ground cinnamon
¼ teaspoon ground cloves
¼ teaspoon ground nutmeg
finely grated rind 1 lemon or lime
2 tablespoons lemon or lime juice

Topping
60g butter
¼ cup milk
½ cup brown sugar
½ cup shredded coconut or chopped walnuts

Heat the oven to 160°C. Grease a deep 20cm round cake tin* and line the base with baking paper, then grease again.

Mix together the bicarbonate of soda and water, then pour over the dates and set aside to cool.

In a large bowl, beat the butter and sugar until light and creamy. Whisk in the eggs until light and fluffy.

Fold in the apples or pears, flour, spices, lemon rind and juice and the soaked dates until well combined.

Pour into the prepared tin and bake for approximately 1 hour, or until a metal skewer inserted into the centre comes out clean.

When the cake is close to being cooked, make the topping as follows:

Combine the butter, milk, brown sugar and coconut or walnuts in a saucepan. Bring to the boil, stirring, and simmer for 2 minutes, stirring constantly, or until the butter and sugar have melted and the mixture is thick.

When the cake is cooked, remove from the oven and spread the prepared topping over the top. Return to the oven and bake for a further 10 minutes, or until the topping is golden brown.

* *If possible, it is best to use a springform cake tin — otherwise you risk losing some of the topping when the cake is turned out.*

STEAMED FRUIT PUDDING

Serves 6

1 teaspoon bicarbonate of soda
¼ cup milk
2 cups fresh breadcrumbs
½ cup chopped dried figs
½ cup chopped dates
½ cup sultanas
½ cup chopped raisins
¼ cup sherry or brandy
½ teaspoon mixed spice
½ teaspoon ground cinnamon
2 teaspoons marmalade
2 ripe bananas, mashed

Grease a 4-cup capacity pudding basin.

Thoroughly mix all the ingredients together in a large bowl and then pour into the prepared basin. Cover the basin with its lid or if it does not have a lid use foil, crimped tightly around the rim and tied in place with kitchen string. Place in a large saucepan, then pour boiling water into the saucepan to a depth of 3cm up the sides of the basin.

Place the lid on the saucepan and simmer on a low heat for 2 hours. Check from time to time that the water has not evaporated from around the basin; if it is getting low replenish with more boiling water.

Take the basin out of the saucepan. Remove the lid or foil and leave the pudding to stand in the basin for 5 minutes, then invert it onto a plate.

Serve wedges of pudding with Egg Yolk Custard (page 144).

Citrus Marmalade

Makes approximately 1.5kg

This recipe is handy when there are a couple of pieces of citrus fruit left in the fruit bowl, looking like they are going to waste. Use them to make this delicious marmalade.

> **500g citrus fruit – for preference include an orange, tangelo or mandarin**
> 1 lemon
> 4 cups water
> 2 cups orange juice or extra water
> 1.5kg sugar

Mince the fruit or chop very finely. Place in a large saucepan and add the water and orange juice or extra water. Bring to the boil and boil briskly for about 25 minutes, or until the peel is soft.

Add the sugar and bring to the boil, stirring until sugar is dissolved. Continue to boil briskly for 25 minutes, or until setting point is reached. To test for setting point, place 2 teaspoons of the mixture on a cold saucer and place in the fridge for a few minutes. Remove the saucer from the fridge and run your finger through the cold marmalade; if the surface is quite firm and wrinkles when you pull your finger through it, the marmalade has reached setting point.

Allow to stand for 10 minutes before pouring the marmalade into warm sterilised jars* and sealing immediately.

* *To sterilise jars: place clean jars in the oven, turn the oven to 100°C and bring up to temperature, then turn off the oven and leave the jars in the oven for 10 minutes.*

Orange Cake

Serves 8

This cake is nice if iced with a little orange or lemon glace icing.

1 orange
125g butter
¾ cup sugar
2 eggs
2 cups self-raising flour
⅔ cup milk
1¼ cups icing sugar, sieved
1 teaspoon softened butter
3 teaspoons (approximately) boiling water

Heat the oven to 160°C. Grease a 20cm round tin and line the base with baking paper, then grease again.

Cut the orange in half and remove any pips. If you plan to ice the cake, first grate 1 teaspoon of orange rind from the orange and squeeze 2 teaspoons of juice. Set aside. Mince or purée the rest of the orange in a food processor.

In a large bowl, beat the butter and sugar until light and fluffy, then whisk in the eggs. Fold in the flour, milk and orange purée all at once and mix until smooth. Pour into the prepared tin and bake for 40 minutes, or until a metal skewer inserted into the centre comes out clean.

Allow to stand in the tin for 5 minutes, then turn out onto a wire rack and invert the right way up to cool.

To make the icing, mix together the icing sugar, softened butter, reserved orange rind and juice and enough boiling water to make a smooth spreading consistency. Using a flat-blade knife occasionally dipped in very hot water, spread the icing over the cooled cake.

Store in an airtight container for up to 5 days.

STEWED OR PURÉED FRUIT

Pork-a-Leekie

Serves 4

3 tablespoons oil
600g pork fillets
180g leek, white part only, finely sliced
1½ tablespoons stewed apple
2 cups chicken stock

Heat 2 tablespoons of the oil in a frying pan over medium-high heat. Brown the pork fillets on all sides, then cover and cook until just tender. Remove from the pan and keep warm.

Pour remaining oil into the pan and sauté the leek over medium heat until softened, stirring often. Add the apple and chicken stock, bring to the boil, then cook for 10 minutes, or until the sauce is reduced by half. Sieve and add salt and white pepper to taste.

Serve the pork fillets sliced and drizzled with the leek and apple sauce.

APPLE AND GINGER PANDOWDY

Serves 4–6

60g brown sugar
120g butter
1½ cups (approximately) stewed apple
1 tablespoon golden syrup
1 egg
¼ cup sugar
¼ cup milk
150g self-raising flour
2 teaspoons ground ginger

Heat the oven to 170°C. Grease a 20cm casserole dish.

In a small saucepan, melt together the brown sugar and 60g of the butter. Pour into the base of the casserole dish. Spoon the stewed apple over this.

Place the remaining 60g butter and golden syrup in the saucepan and melt over low heat.

Meanwhile, in a large bowl whisk the egg and sugar together until smooth. Add the milk, then fold in the flour, ginger and golden syrup-butter mixture. Pour evenly over the apples and smooth out gently.

Bake for 30–35 minutes or until a metal skewer inserted into the centre comes out clean.

Serve with vanilla ice cream or Brown Bread Ice Cream (page 21).

FRUIT CRISP

Serves 4

Any sort of stewed fruit can be used in this recipe; just make sure it is not too liquid. If it is too liquid, bring the fruit to the boil and thicken with some cornflour paste made with 3 teaspoons of cornflour mixed to a paste with approximately 2 tablespoons of cold water (you may not need to use it all).

2 cups stewed fruit, sweetened to taste
45g butter, softened
¼ cup sugar
3 teaspoons honey
2 cups cornflakes

Heat the oven to 150°C. Grease 4 x 1-cup capacity ramekins or an 18cm casserole dish.

Divide the fruit between the ramekins, or pour into a casserole dish.

Whisk together the butter, sugar and honey until well combined, then fold in the cornflakes. Spoon evenly over the stewed fruit.

Bake for 10–15 minutes, or until the topping is golden and crunchy.

Serve with ice cream or whipped cream.

FRUIT FOOL

Serves 2–4

Any type of stewed or puréed fruit can be used in this recipe – my personal favourite is stewed apricots. The recipe can be doubled many times, according to the amount of fruit you have on hand.

> 1 cup thickened cream
> **1 cup stewed fruit, sweetened to taste**

Whip the cream in a bowl until firm peaks form then fold in the fruit until well combined.* Spoon into serving glasses.

VARIATION

Fresh puréed berries can be substituted for the stewed fruit.

* *If extra sweetness is needed, add sifted icing sugar to taste.*

MINI FRUIT CRUMBLES

Serves 4

2 cups stewed fruit, sweetened to taste
½ cup self-raising flour
¼ cup brown sugar, firmly packed
1 tablespoon butter, softened

Heat the oven to 170°C. Grease 4 x 1-cup capacity ramekins and divide the fruit between them.

In a bowl mix together the flour and brown sugar, then rub in the butter with the fingertips until the mixture resembles breadcrumbs. Sprinkle over the top of the fruit.

Bake for 20 minutes, or until the topping is lightly browned and crisp.

SPICED APPLE CAKES

Makes 12

125g butter
1 cup sugar
1 teaspoon grated lemon rind
2 eggs
2 cups self-raising flour
¾ cup milk
2 teaspoons ground ginger
½ teaspoon ground cinnamon
¼ teaspoon ground cloves
½ teaspoon vanilla extract or essence
¼ cup stewed apple

Icing (optional)
60g butter
1 tablespoon golden syrup
200g icing sugar
¾ teaspoon ground ginger
2 teaspoons (approximately) lemon juice

Heat the oven to 160°C. Line 12 x ½-cup capacity muffin tins with paper cases.

In a bowl cream the butter, sugar and lemon rind until light and fluffy then whisk in the eggs. Fold in the flour, milk, spices and vanilla all together.

Place a dessertspoon of mixture in the base of each paper case. Press a small indent into the centres with a wet fingertip or spoon (do not go through to the base) and fill each indent with ½ teaspoon of the apple. Cover with another dessertspoonful of mixture, making sure the apple is covered.

Bake for 20 minutes, or until cooked through.

Remove the cakes from the tins and cool completely on a wire rack.

To make the icing, melt the butter and golden syrup over a low heat. Mix in the icing sugar and ginger and enough lemon juice to make a smooth icing.

Spread a little icing on each of the cooled cakes.

DRIED FRUIT

Collect small amounts of leftover dried fruits and put in an airtight jar until you have enough to make one of the following recipes. See also the recipe for Rock Cakes (page 50) that needs small quantities of dried fruit.

MUESLI

Makes about 4 cups

Any small amounts of cereal can be added to this muesli. It is a great way to use up bits and pieces of all the ingredients on the list.

1 cup rolled oats
½ cup All Bran or similar
½ cup other leftover cereal (such as crushed breakfast
    Wheat biscuits, cornflakes)
2 tablespoons desiccated coconut
2 tablespoons oat bran
½ cup chopped nuts or slivered almonds
1 cup chopped assorted dried fruits

Mix all the ingredients together and store in an airtight container.

Serve with fresh or stewed fruit and yoghurt.

BAKED APPLES

Serves 4

This recipe can be cooked in a regular oven, but it will take up to an hour. This is one of the few recipes I cook in the microwave.

> 4 cooking apples, cored
> **½ cup dried fruit, any sort**
> 30g butter, cut into 4 pieces
> ⅓ cup golden syrup or honey
> ⅓ cup water

If you are not going to use the microwave, heat the oven to 160°C.

Cut a slit into the skin around the 'equator' of each apple (this prevents the apple from exploding).

Place in a ceramic pie dish.

Fill the centre of each apple with the dried fruit of your choice.

Top with a small piece of butter.

Drizzle the golden syrup over the apples.

Pour the water into the base of the dish.

Cook in the microwave on High for 8–10 minutes, or until apples are tender. If baking in the oven, cook for 45–55 minutes, or until the apples are tender.

Serve with vanilla ice cream.

RATAFIAS

sultanas
brandy

Place the sultanas in a jar and cover with brandy. You can keep adding to the jar at any time. Check after a day or two to see that the sultanas remain covered, and if not, add more brandy.

Traditionally, Ratafias are served on toothpicks as an after-dinner treat. They are also good added to ice cream, a cheesecake or fruit mince.

VARIATION

You can also add fresh fruit if you have some spare; just make sure the fruit is well covered with brandy and add 2 teaspoons of sugar for every 125g of fresh fruit.

This makes a delicious topping for ice cream.

TIPSY FRUITIES

Makes about 15

150g dark chocolate
⅓ **cup dried fruits, chopped to the size of sultanas**
1½ **tablespoons roughly chopped nuts or slivered**
      almonds
1 teaspoon marmalade

Line a baking tray with baking paper.

Melt the chocolate in a bowl over a saucepan of simmering water but do not let the water touch the base of the bowl.

Remove the bowl from the saucepan and mix the rest of the ingredients into the melted chocolate.

Place rounded teaspoonfuls of mixture on the tray and leave until they are set.

PEELS AND THINGS

I am loath to waste skins and peels of fruits as they contain valuable vitamins and, in many cases, essential oils. The following recipes give some ideas for using them.

I remember when I was a child that the custom was for parents to peel the oranges and throw the skins into the bin. I've since discovered that the skins from citrus fruits are a treasure in the kitchen. You can finely grate the rind and freeze it in small containers for later use in cakes and biscuits, even savoury dishes. You can also use them for making marmalade. I love marmalade, no breakfast is complete without its inclusion, so I now use the skins to make the following recipe. Any type of citrus skins can be used, but I find some can be a bit overpowering, such as mandarin, so I always include at least half of the orange skins to keep the flavour sweet, light and bright.

I absolutely love candied citrus skin as well. Although it takes several days to make, all the steps are easy as can be, and the end result makes a lovely treat to nibble on.

To make your own lemon essence, place peel in a jar and cover with vodka. It will be ready in one month.

I use the cores and skins of quinces to make a very tasty quince jelly that sets well; the same can be done with the peels and cores of cooking apples, such as Granny Smiths, but I would add a cinnamon stick in the initial boiling up for extra flavour.

I also make a sparkling quince drink from the peels and cores.

(See also: Carrot Cake, page 286; Marmalade Lunchbox Slice, page 287.)

ORANGE SKIN MARMALADE

Makes about 900g

If you don't have the full weight of skins for this recipe, you can freeze the skins progressively until you have enough.

> 500g orange skins, minced or very finely chopped
> 5 cups water
> ½ cup lemon juice
> 6 cups sugar

Place the skins, water and lemon juice in a large stainless steel pot and leave to stand overnight. Next day bring to the boil and boil briskly for 30 minutes.

Add the sugar and stir until dissolved, then bring back to the boil and boil briskly until setting point is reached, which will take about 30 minutes. To test for setting point, place 2 teaspoons of the mixture on a cold saucer and place in the fridge for a few minutes. Remove the saucer from the fridge and run your finger through the cold jam; if the surface is quite firm and wrinkles when you pull your finger through it, the marmalade has reached setting point.

Stand for 10 minutes, then pour into sterilised jars* and seal immediately.

* *To sterilise jars: place clean jars in the oven, turn the oven to 100°C and bring up to temperature, then turn off the oven and leave the jars in the oven for 10 minutes.*

Candied Orange or Lemon Peel

Once you have saved the peel from 2 or 3 oranges or lemons, cut away any white pith with a sharp knife, then slice into 3cm strips.

Next, make the brine in the proportion of 2 teaspoons of salt to 2 cups of warm water. You will need to prepare enough brine to completely cover the peel. Add the salt to the water and stir until the salt is dissolved. Pour the brine over the peel, weigh it down with a saucer so the peel remains submerged and leave it to soak for 3 days.

Drain and wash the peel, then place in a saucepan. Cover with cold water, bring to the boil and cook gently for 2 hours, or until the peel is tender. Drain.

Make enough syrup to cover the peel, using 500g of sugar to 1 cup of water. Place the sugar and water in a saucepan, bring to the boil and simmer for 5 minutes. Pour this syrup over the peel, weigh it down with a saucer and allow it to stand for 3 days.

Drain off the syrup and bring it to the boil. Add the peel and simmer for about 30 minutes, or until the peel is transparent.

Remove the peel from the syrup and place in a single layer on a wire rack over flat trays. Sprinkle a little caster sugar over both sides of the peel. Put in a warm place to dry, or put in the oven at a very low temperature (no more than 60°C fan forced) until dry. Remove from the oven and cool. Store in sealed airtight jars for up to 3 months.

QUINCE JELLY FROM PEELS AND CORES

Use quince jelly as a topping on toast or scones, but also add
½–1 teaspoon to a gravy or casserole – it gives them a wonderful flavour.

375g–1.5kg quince peel and cores
juice of 1 lemon
sugar

Place the peels and cores with the lemon juice in a saucepan and barely
cover with water. Bring to the boil and simmer for 30 minutes. Strain
through a colander, then a kitchen sieve lined with muslin (or even a tea
towel will do).

In a saucepan, add 1 cup of sugar to each cup of liquid. Bring to the boil,
stirring often and cook steadily for about 25 minutes or until setting point
is reached. To test for setting point, place 2 teaspoons of the mixture on a
cold saucer and place in the fridge for a few minutes. Remove the saucer
from the fridge and run your finger through the cold jelly; if the surface is
quite firm and wrinkles when you pull your finger through it, the jelly has
reached setting point.

Pour into warm sterilised jars* and seal immediately.

* *To sterilise jars: place the clean jars in the oven, turn the oven to 100°C and*
bring up to temperature, then turn off the oven and leave the jars in the oven for
10 minutes.

SPARKLING QUINCE

Makes about 3.5 litres

I bottle the sparkling quince in used PET bottles as they have more 'give'. They can also be purchased from home brewing suppliers.

875g quince peel and cores, roughly chopped
875g sugar
1 lemon, diced
18 cups water
11 tablespoons white or cider vinegar

Place all the ingredients in a food-safe bucket and mix well. Place a tea towel over the top and leave to stand at room temperature for 2 days.

Strain first through a colander, then through a fine sieve lined with muslin. Pour into bottles and seal immediately.

In 7–14 days you will have a sparkling quince drink which is absolutely delicious. It's a good idea to refrigerate the drink for a few hours before opening.

Scrapings From the Jar or Tin

All too often it is tempting to throw out the dregs of the contents of jars or tins. When I was young in the days before decimal currency, a friend's thrifty mother had the saying, 'Look after the pennies, and the pounds will look after themselves'. This principle can certainly be applied to the scrapings from jars and tins.

Most spreads are costly to purchase, so there is good economic reason for making the most of jar and tin scrapings by incorporating them into other dishes, snacks or treats.

For instance, a small amount of jam may well go mouldy in the jar, exposed as it is to air after opening. Yet before it gets to that stage, it can be made good use of in cakes, biscuits or even savoury dishes, as the following recipes show.

The contents of the Vegemite or similar spread need not be wasted. If you put about one third of a cup of hot water in the jar and shake it about, it makes an instant type of stock that can be added to casseroles, stews, hotpots and gravies.

Peanut butter is a good addition to or a basis for a satay sauce, and adds extra flavour to a curry. It is a good inclusion in biscuits as well.

Honey, golden syrup and marmalade can similarly be used up in a variety of sweet and savoury applications. Even condensed milk can find its way into biscuits and slices or be added to salad dressings or replace some of the sugar in custard.

CONDENSED MILK

CREAMY MILK BISCUITS

Makes about 18–20

Store any leftover condensed milk in a sealed jar in the fridge. It will keep well for several weeks.

125g butter
½ cup sugar
2 tablespoons condensed milk
1 cup self-raising flour

Heat the oven to 150°C. Line 3 baking trays with baking paper.

Cream the butter and sugar together in a bowl. Mix in the condensed milk, then the flour until well combined.

Place teaspoonfuls of the mixture on the prepared trays, allowing room between them for spreading. Bake for 12–15 minutes, or until light golden. Allow to cool on the trays for 5 minutes, then transfer to a wire rack to cool completely.

CHOC CHIP COOKIES

Makes about 24

125g butter
50g brown sugar
2 tablespoons condensed milk
¼ teaspoon vanilla essence
1 cup plain flour
1 teaspoon baking powder
90g choc chips

Heat the oven to 150°C. Line 2 x 30cm square baking trays with baking paper.

In a large bowl, cream the butter and sugar, then whisk in the condensed milk and vanilla. In another bowl, combine the flour and baking powder then fold into the condensed milk mixture until well combined. Mix in the choc chips.

Allow to stand for 5 minutes, then roll teaspoonfuls of the mixture into balls and place on the prepared trays, evenly spaced and allowing room for spreading. Flatten slightly with a fork that is dipped regularly in flour, or with slightly damp hands.

Bake for 12–14 minutes or until golden brown. Remove the cookies from the trays to cool on a wire rack. Store in an airtight container for up to 2 weeks.

EASY SWEET MAYONNAISE

Makes 1 cup

This recipe can be multiplied out many times if desired. It is a version of a mayonnaise that became every housewife's friend back in the 1970s. We used to use it in potato salads or drizzled over a simple lettuce and tomato salad.

Some people are still very partial to it. It is sweeter than most mayonnaises of today, but for ease of preparation there is nothing like it, and it keeps for ages in a jar in the fridge.

> ½ **cup condensed milk**
> ½ cup white or cider vinegar
> pinch of salt
> ¼ teaspoon mustard powder.

Mix all the ingredients together and leave to stand for 5 minutes, during which time the mayonnaise will thicken.

Store in a jar in the fridge for 4–6 weeks.

SIMPLE LEMON SPREAD

Makes ½ cup

This lemon butter is a wonderful standby as a filling for little cooked tart cases. It is also nice spread on a slice of bread or on a scone. It reminds me of one of my Dad's favourite snacks – condensed milk on generously buttered fresh white bread.

½ cup condensed milk
1 tablespoon lemon juice
½ teaspoon finely grated lemon rind

Mix all the ingredients together well and leave to stand for 5 minutes until the mixture thickens.

Store in a jar in the fridge for up to 3 weeks.

GOLDEN SYRUP

(See also Marmalade Loaf, page 284.)

GOLDEN SYRUP DUMPLINGS

Serves 4

1 cup self-raising flour
pinch of salt
25g butter
1 egg, lightly whisked
1½ tablespoons golden syrup
125g brown sugar
30g butter, extra
1¼ cups water
1 tablespoon lemon juice, optional

In a bowl mix together the flour and salt then rub in the butter with the fingertips until the mixture resembles fine breadcrumbs. With a metal spoon, mix in the egg and, if needed, a little cold water to make a soft dough. Set aside.

In a medium saucepan, bring the golden syrup, sugar, butter, water and lemon juice to the boil.

Drop walnut sized balls of dough into the boiling syrup. Place a piece of greased baking paper over the top of the saucepan, greased side down, place the lid on the pot and simmer for 12 minutes.

Serve immediately with whipped cream or ice cream.

Monte Carlos

Makes about 20

125g butter
125g sugar
3 teaspoons golden syrup
1 egg
1 tablespoon desiccated coconut
250g self-raising flour

Icing
60g butter
1½ cups icing sugar
½ teaspoon vanilla extract or essence
boiling water
⅓ **cup firm set raspberry or other red jam**

Heat the oven to 150°C. Line 3 x 30cm baking trays with baking paper.

Cream the butter, sugar and golden syrup in a large bowl. Whisk in the egg, then fold in the coconut and flour. Roll rounded teaspoonfuls of the mixture into balls and place on the prepared trays, allowing room between them for spreading. Press down lightly with a floured fork. Bake for 12–15 minutes, or until light golden.

Allow to cool on the trays for 5 minutes, before removing to a wire rack to cool completely.

To make the icing, soften the butter then mix in the icing sugar, vanilla and enough boiling water, a few drops at a time, to make a smooth spreading consistency.

Spread the jam on one half of the biscuits and about half a teaspoon of the icing on the remaining biscuits, then pair up the jam biscuits with the iced biscuits and join together.

HONEY

If the honey in a jar has solidified, reheat in the microwave on Medium in 20-second bursts until it melts.

HONEY AND CORNFLAKE DREAMS

Makes about 18–20

90g butter, softened
½ cup sugar
1 tablespoon honey
½ cup chopped raisins
4 cups cornflakes

Heat the oven to 150°C. Line 18 x ¼-cup capacity patty tins with paper cases.

In a bowl cream together the butter, sugar and honey. Mix in the raisins and cornflakes until well combined. Spoon into the paper cases.

Bake for 10 minutes, or until golden.

VARIATION

Drizzle melted dark or white chocolate decoratively over the cooled biscuits.

APPLE CRISP

Serves 4–6

6 cooking apples (such as Granny Smiths)
¼ cup water
1 tablespoon lemon juice (optional)
¼ cup (approximately) sugar

Topping
90g butter
¼ cup sugar
1 tablespoon honey
½ teaspoon ground cinnamon
4 cups cornflakes

Heat the oven to 170°C. Grease a 20cm pie or casserole dish.

Peel and core the apples and cut into small pieces. Place in a saucepan with the water and lemon juice. Bring to the boil, then simmer until the apples are soft, stirring often. Add sugar to taste. Pour into the prepared casserole dish.

Meanwhile to make the topping, melt the butter, sugar and honey together, then mix in the cinnamon and cornflakes until well combined. Spoon the mixture evenly over the apples.

Bake for 20 minutes, or until the topping is crisp.

Serve with vanilla ice cream.

HONEY BISCUITS

Makes about 24

125g butter
1½ tablespoons honey
1 cup sugar
1 egg
⅓ cup desiccated coconut
1½ cups self-raising flour

Melt the butter and honey in a saucepan over low heat, then whisk in the sugar and egg. Fold in the coconut and flour and mix until combined

Roll teaspoonfuls of mixture into balls and place on the prepared trays. Press down lightly with a floured fork. Bake for 12 minutes, or until the biscuits are golden. Cool on the trays for a few minutes, then transfer to a wire rack to cool completely.

HONEY CAKES

Makes about 24

The recipe for these unusual little cakes comes from my paternal grandmother. She worked in the family's bakery in Hobart when she was young. This is one of those treasured recipes from that time that she passed down to me. I make them in scoop patty tins. They don't rise to a point as many little cakes do – therefore I invert them, cut them in half and fill them with sweetened whipped cream. They are a cross between a sponge and shortcake and are wonderful with a cup of tea or coffee.

Tasmanian leatherwood honey makes them truly exceptional.

90g butter
2 tablespoons honey
90g sugar
2 eggs
280g self-raising flour
½ teaspoon bicarbonate of soda
sifted icing sugar, extra for dusting

Cream Filling
1 cup pouring or thickened cream
1 rounded teaspoon icing sugar
¼ teaspoon vanilla extract or essence

Heat the oven to 160°C. Grease 18 scoop patty tins.

Cream the butter, honey and sugar in a bowl, then whisk in the eggs and fold in the combined sifted flour and bicarbonate of soda. Place 1 scant dessertspoon of mixture into each of the prepared patty tins.

Bake for approximately 12 minutes or until a metal skewer inserted into the centre comes out clean.

Remove from the oven, stand in the tins for 4 minutes, then turn out onto a wire rack to cool completely.

To make the cream filling, beat together the cream, icing sugar and vanilla until firm peaks form.

When the cakes are cold, cut in half and fill them with the sweetened whipped cream. Dust the tops with the sifted icing sugar.

HONEY SNAPS

Makes about 40

For this recipe, the cup measurements given should be just under a level cupful, in fact more like ⅞ cup. This ensures lovely crisp little biscuits, delicious with a cup of tea or coffee, a lunch box treat or as a 'dunker' for a cup of tea.

For a pronounced honey flavour, use leatherwood honey.

> 1 scant cup plain flour
> 1 scant cup sugar
> 1 scant cup desiccated coconut
> 1 scant cup rolled oats
> 125g butter
> **1 rounded tablespoon honey**
> 1 teaspoon bicarbonate of soda
> 3 tablespoons boiling water
> ½ teaspoon vanilla extract or essence

Heat the oven to 150°C. Grease 4 baking trays or line with baking paper.

In a large bowl, mix together the flour, sugar, coconut and oats.

Melt the butter and honey in a small saucepan over low heat.

Dissolve the bicarbonate of soda in the boiling water.

Mix the butter and honey mixture and the bicarbonate of soda mixture into the dry ingredients, together with the vanilla, and mix well. Allow the mixture to stand for 5 minutes.

Roll heaped teaspoonfuls of the mixture into balls and place on the prepared trays, allowing ample room between them for spreading.

Bake for 12–15 minutes or until golden. Allow to cool on the tray for 5 minutes, before removing to a wire rack to cool completely.

STIR-FRY MARINADE FOR ANYTHING

This delicious stir-fry marinade is great for beef, pork, chicken or lamb. Simply cut the meat into strips and marinate it in the following mixture for 30 minutes or even up to several hours. The amount of meat needed will depend on the number you are feeding – you can use anything from 500g, which will serve 4 with steamed rice, through to a kilogram or more, which will feed a multitude.

You can use less honey if you like, even 2 or 3 teaspoons will do. You can also reduce the brown sugar if preferred. For my taste however, the following combination is perfect.

   1 clove garlic, crushed
   1 teaspoon grated green ginger root
   ¼ cup soy sauce
   ¼ cup vinegar
   ¼ cup tomato sauce (ketchup)
   1½ tablespoons sweet chilli sauce (optional)
   1 level tablespoon brown sugar
   1 scant tablespoon honey

Mix the marinade ingredients all together. Add the meat to be marinated and leave for at least 1 hour and longer if possible.

Drain off the marinade (reserving it for later) and stir-fry your meat briefly in a hot wok or frying pan. Add any vegetables and stir-fry until almost tender. Add the reserved marinade, bring it to the boil and cook for about 2 minutes. If you would like the sauce a little thicker, mix 2–3 teaspoons of cornflour with about 1 tablespoon of cold water and stir into the mixture at the end of cooking time.

JAM

(See also Monte Carlos, page 271.)

COCONUT JAM TARTLETS

Makes about 24

2 sheets frozen shortcrust pastry or homemade sweet
    shortcrust pastry (see below)
2 rounded tablespoons (approximately) jam, any sort
60g butter
60g sugar
1 egg, lightly beaten
60g desiccated coconut
½ teaspoon vanilla extract or essence or ¼ teaspoon almond
    essence

Heat the oven to 160°C. Grease 24 scoop patty tins.

Cut the pastry into rounds to fit the patty tins (re-roll pastry scraps if
necessary). Fit the rounds into the prepared tins.

Place ½ teaspoon of the jam into each pastry case.

Cream the butter and sugar in a bowl, then mix in the egg, coconut and
vanilla until well combined.

Place a teaspoonful of the coconut mixture into the tarts and bake for
12–15 minutes until golden.

Sweet Shortcrust Pastry
125g butter
125g sugar
1 egg
180g plain flour
70g self-raising flour

In a bowl cream the butter and sugar together until light, then whisk in the egg. Fold in the combined flours and mix with a metal spoon until well combined and the mixture forms a soft dough.

Wrap in cling wrap and place in the fridge for 30 minutes before rolling out on a lightly floured surface.

CURRIED BEEF PIE

Serves 4

The jam in this recipe gives a lovely touch of sweetness to the curry.

    1 tablespoon oil
    500g minced beef
    2 teaspoons curry powder
    1 onion, diced
    1 carrot, diced
    3 teaspoons apricot or plum jam
    1 tablespoon tomato sauce (ketchup)
    2 teaspoons Worcestershire sauce
    2 teaspoons soy sauce
    2 teaspoons chutney
    1 cup water
    ½ teaspoon salt
    3 teaspoons cornflour mixed to a paste with ¼ cup of cold
        water.
    1 sheet frozen puff pastry, thawed

Heat the oven to 200°C. Grease a 20cm casserole or pie dish.

Heat the oil in a large saucepan over medium-high heat. Add the mince and cook until well coloured, stirring often. Mix in the curry powder and continue to cook for 2 minutes.

Stir in the prepared vegetables and cook gently for a further 5 minutes.

Add the jam, sauces, chutney, water and salt and cook for 20 minutes. Stir in enough of the cornflour paste to reach the desired consistency.

Pour into the casserole or pie dish.

Top with the sheet of puff pastry. Prick the pastry in several places with a fork.

Bake for 20 minutes, or until pastry is well risen and golden.

RASPBERRY ROLY POLIES

Makes about 18

1 cup plain flour
1 teaspoon baking powder
¼ cup sugar
2 dessertspoons butter, cut into small pieces
1 egg, lightly beaten
1 teaspoon finely grated lemon rind
a little milk
½ cup firm set raspberry jam or any sort of firm set jam

Heat the oven to 170°C. Line 2 baking trays with baking paper.

Mix the flour, baking powder and sugar together in a bowl. Rub in the butter with the fingertips until the mixture resembles breadcrumbs, or alternatively, place flour, sugar, baking powder and butter in a food processor and process until well combined, then transfer to a mixing bowl.

With a metal spoon, mix in the egg, lemon rind and enough milk to bring the dough together.

Roll out to rectangular shape approximately 8mm thick on a lightly floured surface.

Spread with the raspberry jam and roll up from the longer side.

Cut into 1cm slices and place on the baking trays, cut side up.

Bake for 12–15 minutes, or until lightly browned. Leave to cool on the trays.

SNICKERDOODLES

Makes about 24

The crunchy spice coating makes these biscuits especially tasty.

125g butter
½ cup sugar
1 egg
1½ cups self-raising flour
1 tablespoon sugar, extra
2 teaspoons ground cinnamon
½ teaspoon ground nutmeg
2 tablespoons (approximately) jam, any sort

Heat the oven to 160°C. Grease 3 baking trays or line with baking paper.

Cream the butter and sugar in a bowl, then add the egg and whisk until well combined. Fold in the flour and mix with a metal spoon until a smooth dough is formed.

Mix together the extra sugar, cinnamon and nutmeg in a small bowl. Roll teaspoonfuls of the dough into balls and roll each in the spice mixture. Place on the prepared trays, allowing room between them for spreading.

With your thumb, make an indent in each biscuit but be careful not to go right through. Fill with a little of the jam.

Bake for 12–15 minutes or until golden. Cool on the trays for 5 minutes, then remove to a wire rack to cool completely.

STEAMED JAM PUDDING

Serves 4–6

2 tablespoons jam, any sort
90g butter, softened
grated rind 1 lemon
½ cup sugar
1 egg
1½ cups self-raising flour
2 tablespoons lemon juice
3 tablespoons milk

Grease a 4-cup capacity pudding basin. Line the base with a piece of baking paper cut to fit, and grease again. Place the jam in the bottom of the basin.

In a bowl whisk the butter, lemon rind and sugar together until well combined, then whisk in the egg. Fold in all at once the flour, lemon juice and milk. Pour this batter over the jam.

Place a lid on the basin, or cover with foil and crimp, then tie with kitchen string around the edge to seal tightly.

In a saucepan large enough to hold the basin, pour in water to a depth of 3cm and bring to the boil. Once boiling, put the pudding basin in and place the lid on the saucepan. Reduce the heat to low and simmer for 1½ hours. Check occasionally to ensure that the water is not getting low; if it is, top it up to the original level with boiling water.

Remove the basin from the saucepan. Allow to stand for 5 minutes, then invert the pudding onto a plate.

Serve with Egg Yolk Custard (page 144).

VARIATION

Substitute marmalade for the jam.

MARMALADE

(See also Steamed Jam Pudding variation, page 283.)

MARMALADE LOAF

Makes 1 large loaf

This loaf is delicious sliced and spread with butter. Alternatively, it can be served warm as a dessert with custard.

    3 tablespoons golden syrup
    ¾ cup warm milk
    1 tablespoon marmalade
    1 tablespoon melted butter
    1 cup currants
    1 cup raisins or sultanas
    1 small apple, grated
    2 cups self-raising flour
    ½ teaspoon baking powder
    grated rind 1 lemon

Heat the oven to 160°C. Grease a 13cm x 21cm (approximately) loaf tin and line the base with baking paper, then grease again.

In a large bowl, dissolve the golden syrup in the milk, then add the rest of the ingredients and mix until well combined.

Pour into the prepared tin and bake for 40 minutes or until a skewer inserted into the centre comes out clean.

Allow to cool in the tin for 5 minutes, then turn out onto a wire rack to cool completely.

Bread and Butter Custard

Serves 4–6

2 slices white bread
2 teaspoons butter
4 teaspoons marmalade
½ cup currants
3 eggs
½–⅔ cup sugar
2 cups lukewarm milk
few drops of vanilla essence
½ teaspoon ground nutmeg
30g butter, extra, cut into 6 pieces

Heat the oven to 140°C. Grease a 20cm casserole dish. Prepare a deep baking dish to fit the casserole dish.

Spread the bread with the butter and marmalade, then cut into 2.5cm squares. Place in the casserole dish, buttered side up. Sprinkle the currants evenly over the top.

Lightly whisk the eggs with the sugar, then mix in the milk and vanilla.

Pour the mixture over the bread and currants. Sprinkle the top with ground nutmeg and dot with the small pieces of butter.

Place the casserole dish into the prepared baking dish and pour cold water around it to a depth of 2.5cm and bake for 1½ hours, or until set.

CARROT CAKE

Serves 8

¾ cup brown sugar, firmly packed
½ cup golden syrup
1 tablespoon marmalade
¾ cup light olive, peanut or canola oil
4 eggs
1¼ cups self-raising flour
1 cup plain flour
3 teaspoons ground cinnamon
1 teaspoon ground ginger
½ teaspoon ground cloves
½ teaspoon ground nutmeg
½ teaspoon bicarbonate of soda
400g finely grated carrot
1 teaspoon finely grated lemon rind

Icing
60g butter, softened
120g cream cheese, softened
2 teaspoons finely grated lemon rind
1½ cups icing sugar
2 teaspoons lemon juice

Heat the oven to 150°C. Grease a 23cm round tin.

To make the cake, in a large bowl whisk together the sugar, golden syrup, marmalade, oil and eggs.

In another bowl, mix together the flours, spices and bicarbonate of soda. Add to the egg mixture with the carrot and lemon rind and combine with a metal spoon.

Pour into the prepared tin and bake for 1½ hours or until a metal skewer inserted into the centre comes out clean. Leave to cool in tin for 20 minutes, then turn out onto a wire rack to cool completely.

To make the icing, place the butter and cream cheese in a bowl and beat with a whisk or wooden spoon until well combined. Stir in the lemon rind, sugar and lemon juice until smooth.

Spread the icing decoratively over the top of the cold cake.

MARMALADE LUNCHBOX SLICE

Makes 16—20 squares

1 cup raw sugar
1 tablespoon marmalade
1 cup desiccated coconut
1½ cups mixed dried fruit
1 teaspoon mixed spice
2 teaspoons grated orange rind
2 eggs, lightly beaten
90g butter, melted

Heat the oven to 150°C. Grease an 18cm x 28cm slab tin.

Mix all the ingredients together in a large bowl. Spoon into the prepared tin and smooth out evenly.

Bake for 25 minutes. Leave to cool in the tin and cut into squares when cold.

PEANUT BUTTER AND VEGEMITE

(See also: Peanut Butter Delights, page 47; Peanut Biscuits, page 48.)

CHICKEN KOFTAS WITH SATAY SAUCE

Serves 4

Koftas
500g chicken mince
1 onion, grated
1 egg, lightly beaten
¾ cup fresh breadcrumbs
¼ teaspoon ground cumin
2 teaspoons soy sauce
1 teaspoon Worcestershire sauce
2 teaspoons tomato sauce (ketchup) or chutney
½ teaspoon salt
¼ cup olive oil for frying

Satay Sauce
1 tablespoon olive oil
1 onion, finely diced
2 cloves garlic, crushed
1 heaped tablespoon peanut butter
1 tablespoon soy sauce
1 tablespoon tomato sauce (ketchup)
1 tablespoon Worcestershire sauce
1 cup coconut milk or chicken stock

To make the koftas, place the mince, onion, egg, breadcrumbs, cumin, sauces and salt in a bowl and mix until well combined. Divide into 8 pieces and shape each into a log 10cm long. Heat the oil in a frying pan over medium-high heat and cook the koftas for about 3 minutes on each side until golden and cooked through. Keep warm.

To make the satay sauce, place the oil in a frying over medium heat and sauté the onion for 3 minutes, then add the garlic and sauté for 1 minute more. Add the peanut butter, sauces and coconut milk or stock. Bring to the boil and cook for 3 minutes or until the sauce has reduced by approximately one quarter.

Serve the koftas on plain steamed or boiled rice or couscous, with the satay sauce drizzled over.

VEGEMITE SWIRLS

Makes 4–6

Although in our house we have always called these Vegemite Swirls, any similar type of yeast or vegetable extract spread could be used. Even a nice chutney can be substituted.

> 2 cups self-raising flour
> ⅛ teaspoon salt
> 2 tablespoons butter
> 2 cups grated tasty cheese
> 1 teaspoon Dijon mustard
> ½ cup water
> **3 teaspoons Vegemite or similar**

Heat the oven to 190°C. Line a scone tray with baking paper.

In a bowl sieve the flour and salt, then using fingertips rub in the butter and 1½ cups of the cheese until it resembles breadcrumbs. Alternatively, process to this stage in a food processor, then transfer to a bowl.

Add the mustard and water and mix with a metal spoon until combined.

Turn out onto a lightly floured surface and knead briefly until smooth. Roll out to a rectangle 1cm thick and spread with the Vegemite. Roll up Swiss-roll-style and cut into 1.5cm pieces.

Place cut side up on the tray, sprinkle with the remaining cheese and bake for 12–15 minutes.

VARIATION

Omit the Vegemite and instead sprinkle a little cheese with 1 cup of chopped ham over the dough, then roll up the dough Swiss-roll-style.

INDEX